what do we
know and
what should we
do about...?

the irish
border

Los Angeles | London | New Delhi
Singapore | Washington DC | Melbourne

Katy Hayward

Los Angeles | London | New Delhi
Singapore | Washington DC | Melbourne

SAGE Publications Ltd
1 Oliver's Yard
55 City Road
London EC1Y 1SP

SAGE Publications Inc.
2455 Teller Road
Thousand Oaks, California 91320

SAGE Publications India Pvt Ltd
B 1/I 1 Mohan Cooperative Industrial Area
Mathura Road
New Delhi 110 044

SAGE Publications Asia-Pacific Pte Ltd
3 Church Street
#10-04 Samsung Hub
Singapore 049483

Editor: Natalie Aguilera
Assistant editor: Ozlem Merakli
Production editor: Katherine Haw
Copyeditor: Neville Hankins
Proofreader: Clare Weaver
Indexer: Charmian Parkin
Marketing manager: George Kimble
Cover design: Lisa Harper-Wells
Typeset by: KnowledgeWorks Global Ltd.

Library of Congress Control Number:
2021935076

**British Library Cataloguing in Publication
data**

A catalogue record for this book is available
from the British Library

ISBN 978-1-5297-7064-3
ISBN 978-1-5297-7065-0 (pbk)

For Elsa and Rosa, cross-border by nature and nurture.

contents

titles in the series

What Do We Know and What Should We Do About Sustainable Living?
Kate Burningham and Tim Jackson

What Do We Know and What Should We Do About Slavery?
Julia O'Connell-Davidson

about the series

Every news bulletin carries stories which relate in some way to the social sciences – most obviously politics, economics and sociology, but also, often, anthropology, business studies, security studies, criminology, geography and many others.

Yet despite the existence of large numbers of academics who research these subjects, relatively little of their work is known to the general public.

There are many reasons for that, but, arguably, it is that the kinds of formats that social scientists publish in, and the way in which they write, are simply not accessible to the general public.

The guiding theme of this series is to provide a format and a way of writing which addresses this problem. Each book in the series is concerned with a topic of widespread public interest, and each is written in a way which is readily understandable to the general reader with no particular background knowledge.

The authors are academics with an established reputation and a track record of research in the relevant subject. They provide an overview of the research knowledge about the subject, whether this be long-established or reporting the most recent findings, widely accepted or still controversial. Often in public debate there is a demand for greater clarity about the facts, and that is one of the things the books in this series provide.

However, in social sciences, facts are often disputed and subject to different interpretations. They do not always, or even often, 'speak for themselves'. The authors therefore strive to show the different interpretations or the key controversies about their topics, but without getting bogged down in arcane academic arguments.

Not only can there be disputes about facts but also there are almost invariably different views on what should follow from these facts. And, in any case, public debate requires more of academics than just to report facts; it is also necessary to make suggestions and recommendations about the implications of these facts.

Thus each volume also contains ideas about 'what we should do' within each topic area. These are based upon the authors' knowledge of the field but also, inevitably, upon their own views, values and preferences. Readers may not agree with them, but the intention is to provoke thought and well-informed debate.

Chris Grey, Series Editor

Professor of Organization Studies

Royal Holloway, University of London

about the author

Katy Hayward is Professor of Political Sociology in Queen's University Belfast and a Senior Fellow in the UK in a Changing Europe think tank, where she leads a project on 'The future and status of Northern Ireland after Brexit'. She is the author of many publications, including a series of research reports (2017–2021) for the Irish Central Border Area Network on the impact of the UK–EU negotiations on the border region. In 2019, she was appointed to the technical expert panel of the UK government's Alternative Arrangements Advisory Group on Brexit. She was named Political Studies Communicator of the year (2019) by the Political Studies Association (UK) and her Twitter account (@hayward_katy) received a special award from the Ewart-Biggs Memorial Prize in 2020 for illuminating and explaining the implications of Brexit for the island of Ireland.

introduction

When you're in danger of losing a thing it becomes precious and when it's around us, it's in tedious abundance and we take it for granted as if we're going to live forever, which we're not. (John McGahern, 2005)

Perhaps the most difficult thing to explain about the Irish border is the importance of its insignificance. After the UK's Brexit referendum of 23 June 2016,[1] a steady stream of European dignitaries came to Ireland to visit the border. And there they posed for remarkably dull photographs. Ambassadors, ministers and diplomats stood at the point in a country lane where a dashed yellow line became a solid white one, or between two road signs giving the speed limit in kilometres per hour then miles per hour. Journalists struggled to make the photo ops anything other than clichéd. But the very invisibility of the border was the thing they were there to point out. Although it was easy to spot on a map, the border was difficult to locate 'on the ground'.[2] People did not give it a second thought when crossing it. As a feature of daily life and conversation, the Irish border could all too easily be forgotten about. The visitors came to pay tribute to the fact that this boundary line was, to all intents and purposes, non-existent. The fact that the Irish border had become one of the most seamless and frictionless borders in the world had come to be taken for granted. After decades of diversions, checkpoints and political obsession, moving, trading and working across the border had become both easy and unremarkable. It was this 'absence' of a border that was felt to be suddenly in danger of being lost – all as a consequence of the actions of the neighbouring country, and all subject now to the UK's exit negotiations with the EU. Quite unexpectedly, people on the island of Ireland were having to explain to British and European observers why it was that the openness of the Irish border was so precious. This proved a more difficult task than we might have imagined it would be.

One could say that it was a sign of the success of the 1998 Good Friday (Belfast) Agreement that too few people had cared to remember how 'hard' the Irish border had been before it. It was a luxury to be able to forget. Indeed, the pro-Leave Secretary of State for Northern Ireland, Theresa Villiers (2016), had gone so far as to claim that there had been no such thing. 'The reality', she said, 'is that there has never been a genuinely hard border enforced between the UK and Ireland, and there would not be one if we leave [the EU]'. The British Army had dismantled the last remnants of its military watchtowers along the Irish border only a decade earlier (Reuters, 2007). That a British government minister could assert that this border was never 'genuinely hard' could only be born of either ignorance or deceit. Whatever the cause, it was a sign of the chasm between those who led the path to Brexit and those who stood, inadvertently, in its way. The Irish border was to become described as a 'stumbling block', 'obstacle' and 'tripwire' in the UK withdrawal negotiations. Yet people on both sides of the border and both sides of the Brexit debate were in full agreement on one fundamental point: they wanted the conditions of its current invisibility to change as little as possible.

The novelist John McGahern, a son of the small border county of Leitrim, intimates in his memoirs that taking something important for granted is as natural and as misguided as our common human failure to acknowledge our own mortality. Just because we let something become 'unthinkable' does not make it any less likely to happen. This, perhaps, is the overriding lesson of Brexit, not least as viewed from the island of Ireland. McGahern's remarks echo Hegel's sombre reflection that humans learn too late: 'The owl of Minerva spreads its wings only with the falling of the dusk.' We can only really begin to understand and – in a meaningful sense – to conceptualise what has occurred when the bustle of activity is over. If the five years of the Brexit process, from referendum campaign to exit from the 'transition period', was characterised by anything, it was confusion and commotion. There was a peculiar intensity to the Brexit process; it so often felt surreal and implausible, even as it unfolded. This is especially true of what came to pass regarding the jointly agreed objective of 'avoiding a hard border on the island of Ireland'.

The subject of 'the Irish border' encapsulated profound differences in 'reality' as viewed by Remainers and Leavers, British and Europeans, Unionists and Nationalists. It is only when the actual consequences of decisions made and actions taken begin to settle that we are able to take it all in. It is a good time to consider afresh the nature of the Irish border, in form and symbol. Although Brexit is far from over (undoing a near-50-year relationship and establishing a new one is a long-term project, after all), the night has closed in on the UK's membership of the EU. And Northern Ireland is left in a tenuous position, both outside and inside the European Union, and both inside and outside the UK's internal market. In effect, the Brexit process has transformed the borders all around this small and awkward region. A book of this nature is a timely opportunity to consider how we might yet act more wisely and philosophically in the era of the Irish border – and Ireland's borders – to come.

What is a border?

Before considering what is particular about the Irish border, it is worth addressing the fundamental matter of what 'a border', or specifically a state border, actually is. In some respects, borders can be the most obvious manifestation of a state and of its power.[3] Think of passport gates at an airport, or customs inspection facilities in a ferry port, or wire fencing 2 metres high stretching for hundreds of kilometres through open countryside. There are few instances when we see the exercise of state control so literally. Borders represent the power of a state, but such power that has only been exercised over that particular territory for a certain period of time. The boundaries of a state denote historical processes of division and consolidation. And if politics is predominantly focused on the exercise of power within the jurisdiction of the state, it is understandable that state borders can also feature prominently in political discourse and identity. That said, the materiality and the symbolism of a border can be of contrasting significance. The post-1998 Agreement Irish border is an example of a border with little importance in terms of its practical effect or visibility, but tremendous significance for political and cultural identity. This leads to the most important point about the nature of a state border: even where it happens to be contiguous with some topological feature of landscape, a state border is always and primarily a product of human, specifically social, behaviour. There can be no 'natural' state borders because there is no 'natural' state.

In and of itself, drawing a line across a map does nothing; it is human activity (including our collective imaginations) which gives a border meaning and effect. From this principle, we know that the significance of any border varies by context. The relevant context, for a state border, is not just geographical; it is historical, legal, political, socio-cultural and economic. Immediately we see, therefore, that there is an awful lot in the meaning of any state border that may be subject to differing interpretation and contestation. That contestation may come from within the state or from another state, as in the case of irredentism – the claim by one state over the territory of another. Furthermore, although borders tend to be seen as emblematic of state power, it is more accurate to see them in terms of the limitations of sovereignty rather than the manifestation of sovereignty. Because, even in the digital age, the jurisdiction of a state is primarily defined in territorial terms: a border constitutes a boundary to the scope of state power. This is where we come to another characteristic of every border, but one which is bizarrely often overlooked: a border has two sides. For a start, what a border means in practice depends very much on the extent of the differences between the rules, practices and norms of the states on either side of it. When something moves across a border, it exits one state and enters another. Most popular discourse about borders assumes that sovereignty is exercised at a border by restricting what can enter a state. But what is being allowed to 'exit' the other state is also key. If economic development or national security, say, depend on what is able to enter a state, they also depend on what other states are willing to allow to leave. If movement across a border is both exit from a state and entry to another, then it demonstrates the connectedness of states more than their separateness.

This leads to another dimension of the two-sided nature of borders which means a limitation on state sovereignty. It is possible for one state alone to make a border 'harder' or more difficult to cross. However, it is not possible for one state by itself to make a border more open – this depends on action (and agreement) on both sides. As such, there is a certain vulnerability associated with a border. Friction imposed by one side of a border has consequences for the other. Ultimately then, although borders are often conceived in terms of division and separation, it is sometimes better to understand them as meeting points. In the case of air and maritime travel, the entry post of an airport or harbour can be the 'meeting point' between countries that are geographically distant. In the case of land borders, the connection is between neighbours, and 'borderlands' can be where their interdependence is most manifest. Following this, a region that runs either side of a border can have a unique character born of the 'meeting' of the two states. Where the relationship between the neighbouring states is positive, there can be particular benefits associated with being in the border region; where the relationship is negative, the border region may suffer particular harm. As one might expect, border regions tend to experience the most direct impact of the existence of a land border. The border region of the island of Ireland is no exception.

There is another dimension to the dualism of a border. The boundary line of a state is of obvious significance; it is the territorial limitation to the rules of a state. However, the actual manifestation of a state's border need not necessarily occur at that boundary line. Indeed, as the exercise of state surveillance and power has become more sophisticated, so 'bordering practices' have diversified too. The effects of a border can take place far from the border line. The meeting point, in such instances, is not between two states but between individuals. This is seen most particularly in immigration enforcement. When a hospital receptionist or an employer or a landlord is required to check on the residency rights of a potential patient, employee or tenant, they are acting as a 'border agent'. It is at such points that the legal terms of the border are put into in practice. Border studies of the twenty-first century increasingly have to account for the ways in which border controls are exercised remotely, often by people other than official enforcers or agencies, or in virtual or digital spheres.

Lastly, on this theme, a border can have different effects for the movement of different types of things. As a consequence, a border can be 'hard' and 'soft' at the one time. To put it in simple terms, a country may have a very tough immigration policy (only allowing the entry of certain groups of people into its territory under strict conditions) at the same time as it has a liberal trade policy (allowing goods to flow in fairly freely). But the manifestation of a border may not only be seen in movement across it. A border may also be 'hard' or 'soft' in its physical manifestation too. A 'hard' border may be evident in the form of border posts, surveillance cameras, watchtowers, inspection facilities. At the same time, that border may be 'soft' in terms of how easily things can move across it.

The history of the Irish border is a good illustration of this. At the same time as the border was heavily fortified in some places as a result of the Troubles (the 30-year period of violent conflict prior to the 1998 Agreement), with military checkpoints and soldier foot patrols and blocked roads, it was quite open in other respects, as the EU's single market came into effect and the movement of goods across it became increasingly unrestricted. All of this complexity goes to show why borders are such a marvellously rich subject for discussion and analysis. It also shows why analysis of any border at any point in time will always be frustratingly incomplete. The scope for any study of a border is, ironically, boundless. This book on the Irish border comes at a point when we have been forced to recognise the endurance of borders (marked by a century of partition) and the weakness of borders (marked by a global pandemic). This paradox runs throughout this book, as I attempt to explain the importance and the unimportance of the Irish border.

Finding common ground

A good place to begin to 'explain' the Irish border would, one imagines, be in identifying its origins. However, herein we immediately encounter the difficulties of the subject. It is not a neutral topic.[4] There are not just different interpretations of where the Irish border comes from – there are competing and contested narratives about it. An Irish nationalist explanation for the Irish border is that it exists because of British colonialism, and it has persisted because of British interference in Ireland. A unionist explanation for the Irish border is that it exists because of the distinctiveness (which may be understood as a form of 'Britishness') of what became Northern Ireland, and that it has persisted because most people there wish to remain in the United Kingdom with Great Britain. For nationalists, the border (and thus Northern Ireland) is, in essence, illegitimate. For unionists, the border is the formal means of assuring them of their legitimate place on the island of Ireland. For unionists, nationalists' wish to see the border removed represents (sometimes less implicitly than others) a desire to see unionism gone too. For nationalists, unionists' reification of the border represents (sometimes less implicitly than others) the brutalisation of the Irish nation. These differences were epitomised in the disagreements that surrounded the centenary of Northern Ireland in 2021. Unionist plans to celebrate Northern Ireland's 100 years were repelled by nationalists, not least because the very existence of Northern Ireland means the partition of Ireland.

As such, contemporary discussion of the Irish border is rarely about the border per se, but about the legitimacy (or otherwise) of unionism in Ireland. By extension, discussion of the Irish border is about the relationship between Britain and Ireland. This has taken on a wholly new significance in the context of the UK's withdrawal from the EU. In particular, the Protocol on Ireland/Northern Ireland that was part of the UK–EU Withdrawal Agreement has brought a new border to the fore: the Irish Sea border. In order to appreciate best the context in which borders all around Northern Ireland are now seen as of greater significance than ever, it is necessary to consider the background context in a way that helps us understand the competing claims of both unionism and nationalism in the present day.

In order to do this it is first necessary to think rather further back than the tumultuous years during and after the First World War. Those years were the culmination of several movements and processes with deep historical roots – ones of resistance to British rule and of resistance to the Catholic Church, to name but two (Hennessey, 1998). Ireland's experience of those years was also particular to their moment – a time when men drew red lines across maps of lands they had never visited, and empires were thus broken and states created. It is also necessary to allow for a nuanced understanding of what the Protocol on Ireland/Northern Ireland in the UK–EU Withdrawal Agreement describes as 'the unique circumstances of the island of Ireland'. These unique circumstances are not contained to the geographical unit of the island; they have been intrinsically shaped by Great Britain, for better and for worse. Taoiseach Garret FitzGerald (30 September 1982) eloquently described 'the deep conviction of Irish nationalists that the island of Ireland is a natural geographical area forming historically a single cultural and political unity'. But, as he well knew, it is erroneous to conflate an island with self-containment, let alone with a singular culture. For many centuries, travel across the sea in a boat would have been quicker and easier than travel across land on foot or by other means. The historical effects of maritime connections of culture and commerce and kinship are no less significant because they are harder for us to appreciate now, in our age of fast road, rail and air passage. As with any border, the Irish Sea can be seen as a line of connection or a bridge between Britain and Ireland as well as a 'natural' boundary.

Finally, it is important to allow for discontinuity in history. Unionism and nationalism as identities and ideologies are concomitant with the emergence of the modern state, and the very concept of nationhood. Yet, because they are both political ideologies fostering a form of ethnonational identity, they trace their origins far beyond this. To outline the 'background' of the Irish border is to proffer some context for the legitimacy claims of both unionism and nationalism. But it is also to show that the events, decisions and assumptions which resulted in the drawing of the Irish border were never predetermined. Just as it was naive of any of us to think, but a few years ago, that the borders around Northern Ireland were fading into perpetual insignificance, so it would be foolish of us now to imagine that there is anything inevitable about the future of the Irish border.

Notes

1. Northern Ireland voted by 56 per cent to remain in the European Union; the UK as a whole (given the proportionately large size of England and Wales) voted 52 per cent to leave the EU.
2. This was memorably described by 'the Irish border' itself through a Twitter account of an anonymous author who tweeted under the pseudonym of @BorderIrish through the ins and outs of the UK's withdrawal from the EU: 'Then the journalists started to show up with all their daft questions: "How did you get here? Are you scared? How do you really feel?" Hiding from British journalists sent by the editors to find me has been the only fun thing about Brexit. They write articles saying they've "straddled" me (I know, the cheek of them) because they love to sound macho, but that actually means they couldn't find me.' (@BorderIrish, 2019: 6)
3. In focusing on a territorial concept of state borders here, I am not neglectful of the critical developments in border studies' literature which focus upon the de-territorialised, multiscalar, symbolic and dynamic nature of borders. This is reflected in the concepts of border 'practices', border 'regimes', 'borderscapes' and 'border mobilities', to name but a few (see, inter alia, Anderson and O'Dowd, 1999; Brambilla et al., 2015; Parker and Vaughan-Williams, 2014; Pickering and Weber, 2006; Sassen, 2006; Scott, 2020; Wilson and Donnan, 2012). This section is intended to incorporate some key insights from that broad literature while necessarily remaining focused on the most pertinent of concepts for this short study.

4. This seems an appropriate point to note that my use of terminology throughout this book does not come in ignorance of the potential for offence to be taken on the part of the reader. No offence is intended, but nor can it be avoided. Some of the most crucial proper nouns for a book on this subject are used (or read) to signify political preference. No such preference, or ignorance of the same, should be taken in the terminology used herein. Unless when citing others, I use the neutral term 1998 Agreement to refer to the Good Friday/ Belfast Agreement. In referring to the northern jurisdiction on the island of Ireland, I use the internationally recognised legal term of Northern Ireland, while I acknowledge that this is contested. And I use both Ireland (as the proper name of the state) and, where necessary to avoid confusion, the Republic of Ireland. I sometimes refer to 'the north' and 'the south', which are in common usage and not meant pejoratively; these are also the nouns used in the 1998 Agreement. Finally, I only capitalise the terms 'unionist' and 'nationalist' where they refer to formalised political parties or movements rather than broad 'communities', identities or sentiment.

background

Myths and mobilities

It is not possible to understand the Irish border without understanding unionism. And it is not possible to understand unionism without appreciating unionists' strong sense of identification with the territory of Ireland. This is a critically important point, and one which is often neglected because it is rarely articulated in this way. The strength and vehemence of unionism comes from an attachment to the land, and related sentiments of belonging, ancestry and bequeathal. The course of history has meant that this attachment tends to be concentrated on the northern part of the island, for reasons I will endeavour to explain. As one would expect, there are foundational myths of unionism as well as nationalism. One such narrative centres upon Uliadh, the north-east of the island, in the pre-Christian era. The Ulster Unionist politician Ian Adamson (1987) produced the most substantive work in support of this narrative. He claimed that there was evidence of ethnic and linguistic difference (in the Ullans language) and of a shared territorial kingdom between the west of Scotland and the north-east of Ireland (the Dalraida, or Dál Riata) (Adamson, 1998). This narrative does not just seek to give unionist identity a connection to Ireland that pre-dates the Celts and Gaels, it also emphasises ancient ties to Scotland across the sea. What is more, Adamson is keen to point to long-existing socio-cultural differences on the island of Ireland and claims that these have taken both territorial and violent forms. For example, he posits that the Black Pig's Dyke (a series of linear earth-works that pre-date the Iron Age and lie across the width of the north midlands and south Ulster) were used for defence against invasion. For some unionist and loyalist communities, 'that ancient frontier between Ulster and the rest of Ireland' legitimises their identity and, by extension, partition (REACH, 2021).

Another historic distinction between territorial areas of the island of Ireland that is seen to have contemporary significance is among its provinces. Now commonly known as a fourfold division of the territory (albeit with no contemporary administrative or politico-legal significance), the Irish word for 'province', *cuigeadh*, indicates that there were once 'five-fifths of Ireland' (MacNeill, 1920). These 'chief kingdoms' are sometimes seen as the original forms of political administration on the island of Ireland. Although they varied in number and did not become formalised as four provinces until the seventeenth century, these broad divisions reach into the pre-Christian era through mythology. The Ulster Cycle creates the impression of a distinctive Ulster province, ruled from Emain Macha (Navan Fort), albeit wracked with internal conflicts. The significance of these myths for current political ideology rests largely in the figure of Cú Chulainn and his 'defence of Ulster' from Queen Medb's Army of Connacht in the Táin Bó Cúailnge (cattle raid of Cooley). He is immortalised in art and culture (not to mention wall murals in Belfast housing estates) that seeks to inspire similar acts of bravery against 'invaders', be they those from elsewhere in Ireland (as per unionist narratives) or from outside Ireland (as per nationalist narratives).

In fact, the population of Ireland was made of peoples who began to arrive on the island about 9,000 years ago (Mallory, 2013). There were, as it is often put, many 'waves' of such 'Irelanders', most of them coming from Britain. It was not until an early form of the Irish language had spread in its use across the island, towards the middle of the first Millennium CE, that a concept of 'Irish' people began to develop. Evidence from art, scholarship and archaeology would show that the Irish and the island of Ireland were intimately connected to the wider world. This was particularly the case through the spread of Christianity, the influence of which not only brought common forms of social organisation and religious belief across the island. Christianity was also at the heart of the cultural, social and political connections built between Ireland and Europe. St Patrick, the founder of Christianity in Ireland, came – or, rather, was brought – from Britain.

The Irish Sea, and the rivers which ran into it, were channels which joined the islands in many ways over many centuries.

> From Late Antiquity to the coming of the vikings, the island's main and most obvious interaction was with Britain. As might be expected, evidence for this interaction is primarily concentrated on the east coast, where personal names, dynastic names, origin legends, saints' names, military alliances and archaeology combine to suggest that the Irish Sea from Scotland to Cornwall was a busy highway. (Bhreathnach, 2018: 16)

The influence during this long period was not just in one direction. Bhreathnach (2018) describes the communities of Ireland in ways which often, either directly or indirectly, include parts of Britain: through kingdoms (as in the Dál Riata), military alliances, marriages and trade, as well as mythology and Christian mission. An important point made by Frame (2018: 524) is that the 'regional character of Ireland's links with the exterior scene is readily apparent'. The distinctiveness of the north-east of Ireland was formed by a maritime zone which, in the Viking age, 'became the centre of an economic and political world extending from Dublin and Anglesey through [the Isle of] Man and the Hebrides back to Bergen and Trondheim' (Frame, 2018: 524). But from the thirteenth century on, it was the influence of the invasion of what Frame (2018: 524) describes as 'aristocrats with close, though sometimes difficult, links to the English and Scottish kings' which was to have a most profound impact on the northern region of the island.

Defence and defiance

The Anglo-Norman invaders exacerbated and exploited the divisions between the regions or provinces of Ireland as they existed in the twelfth century. The foray of mercenaries onto the island of Ireland was at the request of a deposed and resentful king of Leinster. The cost for his regaining provincial power was land and loyalty to an English king. Within a space of a few years, the towns and territory of Ireland became battle sites for contests of royal, military and ecclesiastical power. The rapacious and chaotic nature of the takeover of Irish land was evident in the actions of John de Courcy, an Anglo-Norman knight who took it upon himself to lead a small army northwards to defeat the last Gaelic king of Ulaid, Ruaidhrí

Mac Duinnshléibhe (Duffy, 1995: 3). Even though Henry II, King of England, had not sanctioned his conquest, he subsequently named de Courcy the first Earl of Ulster. Nevertheless, the castles (notably Carrickfergus) and the abbeys the new earl built were in defence from, and defiance of, his Anglo-Norman compatriots. He was defeated and succeeded by Hugh de Lacy, son of the Lord of Meath, in 1205 on Good Friday (the one day of the year he would not wear his armour). The Earldom of Ulster included Uliad, in the north-east, but it was very far from covering the whole of the north of Ireland.

Maps of medieval Ireland may not reveal the internecine battles of those who represented English-based rule in Ireland but they do indicate a long-standing difference between the north-west of Ireland and the rest of the country that took political, social and cultural form. Until the seventeenth century, the north-west of Ireland remained under the rule of Gaelic lords, most notably the Uí Néill (O'Neill) dynasty. The brief incursion of the north-east from Scotland in the early fourteenth century by Edward the Bruce, brother of the Scottish king, was at their invitation. The Gaelic leaders saw potential for mutual benefit from Scottish efforts to reduce the power and land held by the Anglo-Normans. Although the incursion was a failure, the resistance continued. Over time, the contraction of English rule to centre upon the Pale in Leinster was caused by cultural and social factors (e.g. the effects of the Black Death, the 'Gaeliscisation' of certain dynasties) as well as military and political ones. This trend was countered in the sixteenth century with the Tudor conquest of Ireland. The strategy of 'surrender and regrant' used a mix of military force and 'politic drifts and amiable persuasions' (Ellis, 1985: 111). It saw English laws applying in Ireland and land owned by the English Crown but 'returned' to local lords through Royal Charter. The O'Neill dynasty was thus granted the earldom of Tyrone. But the policy of exerting control of Ireland through centralising government in Dublin failed and the results were catastrophically violent. Ulster remained the most resistant to Anglicisation.

The Crown's effort to take Ulster by military conquest provoked what became the Nine Years War in Ireland, in which O'Neill and the other Gaelic chieftains in Ulster fought to retain their autonomy (Morgan, 1993). When their opposition to England combined with resistance to the spread of Protestantism, they were able to ally themselves with England's enemy, Spain. Drawing also upon support from other lords, including some Old English (former Anglo-Norman) dynasties, the Gaelic earls took the military challenge to beyond the boundaries of Ulster at the turn of the seventeenth century. Their efforts failed and they retreated northwards once more, only to head to Europe in 1607 to seek to garner support from Catholic states for another challenge to English Protestant rule in Ireland. The Flight of the Earls ended in failure. Their lands were deemed forfeited to the Crown, and the formal policy of colonisation of the north of the island through the Plantation of Ulster was initiated in 1609. Settlement in the north-eastern part of Ulster by wealthy Scottish Presbyterians had begun a few years previously, but the plantation that took place under James I (VI of Scotland) took land across the whole of Ulster. The new landowners were predominantly Presbyterian and Anglican, from Scotland and England, and they were told not to employ local Irish tenants. The intention was to ensure that Ulster – the part of Ireland historically most resistant to English rule – would be subdued once and for all through dispossession, dispersal and conversion. However, as the Lord Deputy of Ireland, Arthur Chichester, himself wrote in 1610: the native Irish in Ulster were 'generally discontented, and repine greatly at their fortunes, and the small quantity of land left to them' (Rafferty, 1994: 12).

The seventeenth century was one of turbulence and violence in which Ulster formed the battleground for wider conflicts between Catholic and Protestant, Scottish and English, as well as Irish and settlers. The Battle of the Boyne in 1690 – commemorated annually by the Orange Order on 12 July – was a European battle, with soldiers from many countries making up the Jacobite Army of the deposed Catholic King James II (VII) of England and Scotland and the army of the Protestant Dutch King, William of Orange. The battle was not 'decisive' for the island of Ireland. The tensions over religious denomination, political representation, landownership, language and discrimination would endure, and particularly so in Ulster.

The Union

After the creation of the Parliament of Great Britain in 1707, the execu-tive power of the Irish Parliament in effect rested with the British govern-ment in Westminster. The legislative power of the Irish Parliament was further curtailed just over a decade later, with the Dependency of Ireland on Great Britain Act (1719). Resentment grew at the enduring discrimina-tion against both Catholics and Dissenters (including Presbyterians), and this took shape in the form of the Volunteer movement which was inspired by the revolution in America and, later, France. The Constitution of 1782 brought greater legislative and executive powers for the Irish Parliament, but reform happened very slowly in a parliament whose members could only be wealthy Anglicans. The 1798 Rebellion of the United Irishmen sought 'equal representation of all the people' in the government of Ireland. The north-east was a site of major battles, with the United Irishmen being led by Presbyterian Henry Joy McCracken against the combined forces of the British and Irish Army (Power, 1997). The impact of this brief but intense period of violence was made all the greater by the involvement of French soldiers. Fearing that Ireland would once again become a means by which European countries could 'interfere' in British affairs, a merger of the Kingdoms of Britain and Ireland was proposed. Even some former Irish Volunteers welcomed the prospect as a route to reform, by curtailing the dominance of the 'Protestant Ascendancy' in Ireland (Smyth, 2000). The Acts of Union of 1800 passed by the Parliament of Great Britain and the Parliament of Ireland saw the dissolution of the Irish Parliament, and Irish MPs crossing the Irish Sea to take their seats in Westminster. Article One of each Act had that they 'for ever after, be united into one Kingdom, by the Name of The United Kingdom of Great Britain and Ireland'.

The causes of dissatisfaction remained, of course, but now it was necessary to persuade British and Irish MPs of the need for reform. The achievement of Catholic Emancipation in 1829 encouraged mobilisation, under the leadership of Daniel O'Connell, towards repealing the union and addressing systemic poverty in Ireland. The Great Famine (1845–1851) not only revealed catastrophic failure of government, administration and tenure, but forever changed the population of Ireland, with over a million lives lost and a million more emigrating. The internationalisation of Ireland's difficulties came in other ways too. The secret society of the Irish Republican Brotherhood depended considerably on the support and interest of its sister organisation in the United States, Clan na Gael. The formation of the Land League in 1879 was stimulated in part by a fall in agricultural prices in Europe, as well as poor harvests, which left Irish farmers unable to pay rent to landlords. By the late nineteenth century, there were a range of organisations campaigning for major reform in Ireland. One of these was the Home Rule League, which began as a pressure group for self-government in Dublin but quickly became a political party. In its first general election, in 1874, it won 59 seats in Ireland, taking the vast majority of these from the Liberal Party, and making it the third largest party in Westminster

(Jackson, 2003: 29). The political map of Ireland showed a north/south divide in election results, with the Conservative Party consistently doing well in Ulster (and not elsewhere in Ireland). However, any map of election results only tells a partial story: that is, the candidate who came first past the post as voted for by those who had the franchise and who exercised it that day. The electoral picture became a little more representative by the time of the 1885 election.

The Franchise Act (1884) meant that all adult male householders who paid rates had the vote; this tripled the size of the electorate in Ireland (Walker, 2005). The terms of the political debate had also changed. The owner–tenant tensions were no longer the dominant issue of concern to most voters. The Conservative and Liberal Parties campaigned in Ireland as 'unionist' parties. The Conservative Party in particular made efforts to cajole newly enfranchised Protestants by appealing to the Orange Order. Founded 90 years previously in Co. Armagh to defend Protestant interests, the Order was beginning to enjoy something of a revival in reaction against the movements for land reform and Home Rule. It was bolstered by the fact that all Conservative MPs were Protestant (Jackson, 1989). Opposing them was the Irish Parliamentary Party (the new name for the Home Rule League) which now campaigned as a 'nationalist' party under Charles Stewart Parnell. Although he was a Protestant, 80 of the 85 MPs of Parnell's party were Catholic (Walker, 2005). Nationalists also now utilised a new form of grassroots mobilisation in this election. Its effectiveness was aided by the fact that Parnell was also leader of the Irish National League, the successor to the Land League. The Irish Parliamentary Party won 85 seats in the 1885 election, including 17 of the 33 in Ulster and the last seats held by the Liberal Party.

Splits within the Liberal Party, plus frustration at the obstructionist tactics of the large bloc of Irish nationalist MPs in Westminster, helped convince Prime Minister Gladstone of the need to act on Home Rule. However, bringing the question of the union centre stage in Britain was, unsurprisingly, to bring only deeper divisions. The defeat of the Government of Ireland Bill (1886) caused further splits among the Liberals and provoked the calling of another general election. In Ulster, rather than support Gladstone, the vast majority of Liberals chose to lend their support to the Conservatives under the common banner of 'unionist' (Jackson, 1989). Thus Home Rule was now clearly the issue which decided people's voting choice in Ireland. Gladstone lost the election, but shortly after his

Figure 2.1 Results of the 1885 election by parliamentary constituency on the island of Ireland[1]

return to power for a fourth time, he introduced another Home Rule Bill in 1893. It was forced through the House of Commons but defeated in the House of Lords. It was not until two decades later – when John Redmond's Irish Parliamentary Party held the balance of power in the House of Commons – that a third Home Rule Bill was introduced by the Liberal Prime Minister, H. H. Asquith, in 1912. This was a mix of the previous two bills, with a separate Irish Parliament in Dublin and some powers and some seats for Irish MPs reserved in Westminster. The Bill was passed in the Commons but then rejected in the Lords three times between 1912 and 1914. At its third reading in May 1914, which lasted a number of days, the Unionist MP Edward Carson stated:

> I say this to my Nationalist fellow-countrymen, and indeed also to the Government, you have never tried to win over Ulster. You have never tried to understand her position. (Gwynn, 1932: 255)

There can be little doubt that the effect of his message was bolstered by the Ulster Covenant, which he and fellow Ulster Unionist MP, James Craig, had prominently supported (Stewart, 1967). Signed by some 470,000 people convinced that Home Rule would be 'disastrous', the Covenant took different form for men and women, with the former pledged to use 'all means which may be found necessary to defeat the present conspiracy'.[2] At the same time, the efforts of the newly formed Ulster Volunteer Force to arm themselves were widely known (Fitzpatrick, 1996). Nervousness about the ability of Ulster unionists to garner wider sympathy for their cause, and what that might mean for Westminster politics, meant that the British government felt obliged to respond. In July 1914 it submitted an amending bill to the House of Lords (before it had considered the actual Bill) which sought to exclude Ulster from the effect of the Home Rule Act. The bill stated that:

> the Government of Ireland Act, (1914), shall not apply to the excluded area as hereinafter defined. In this Act, the expression 'the excluded area' includes the Province of Ulster'. (Article 1i-ii)

> [And] the words 'Ireland' and 'Irish' shall be construed … as not including the excluded area. (Art 9.i.a)

It was unclear as to whether the exclusion would be temporary. However, the matter soon became moot when war in Europe was declared in August 1914. Asquith abandoned the amending bill and pushed a Suspensory Act instead. This had the effect of suspending the implementation of the Government of Ireland Act (1914), the third attempt at Home Rule for Ireland, at the very same time it received Royal Assent. Not for the first time had British involvement in European conflict changed the course of Irish history.

When did the border begin?

A history of the Irish border could begin at several different points in time. It could start on 23 December 1920 when the Government of Ireland Act became law (HMSO, 1920). This provided for two separate parliaments of self-government in the six north-eastern counties of 'Northern Ireland' and the 26 counties of 'Southern Ireland'. Or perhaps the Irish border began on 3 May 1921, when the Act came into effect. Elections were called for the 24th of that month for both new parliaments in Dublin and Belfast. The Northern Ireland House of Commons first sat on 7 June 1921 and contained 40 Ulster Unionist, six Nationalist Party and six Sinn Féin members (the latter of whom did not take their seats) (Coleman, 2014: 100). That parliament would govern Northern Ireland for the next 50 years, largely from Stormont buildings. However, the southern parliament (124 Sinn Féin members, 4 Independent Unionists) never properly convened (Coleman, 2014; Laffan, 1983). So maybe the Irish border began instead on 6 December 1921, with the signing of the Anglo-Irish Treaty to end the Irish War of Independence. The treaty created the Irish Free State, giving Ireland the same constitutional status as the Dominion of Canada or Commonwealth of Australia. The day after it came into full legal effect in December 1922, with the Irish Free State (Constitution) Act, the Northern Ireland Parliament exercised its right to be excluded. But the Irish border was already in contention. The split among Nationalists (including Sinn Féin) between those who supported the treaty and those who instead wanted to see the all-island independent republic they had declared in 1919 led to the Irish Civil War, June 1922 to May 1923 (Hopkinson, 1988). Did the victory of the pro-Treaty side in the civil war constitute the beginning of the Irish border? Or perhaps it only formally came into existence when the Anglo-Irish Treaty was registered by the Free State at the League of Nations, in

July 1924? Last but far from least stands the thesis that the Irish border was only properly formed in December 1925, when the three heads of government of the Irish Free State, Northern Ireland and the United Kingdom set aside the leaked report of the Irish Boundary Commission, and approved the border as it lay.

What do we learn from the difficulties of pinpointing the beginning of the Irish border? That its history is complicated as well as contested. That negotiators may find innovative arrangements in treaties, but that these can be quite quickly undermined by their political reception or by their incomplete implementation. International treaties may be crucial but not decisive. There can be considerable gaps between the intentions of negotiators and the decisions of politicians left to implement what was agreed. We learn that disagreements over process and priorities within political movements can have lasting effect. We see that the alchemy of a negotiated compromise against the background of fervent national ideology can be volatile. The task of recounting the 'background' to a border becomes considerably more difficult when we allow that any such history is inseparable from the historical narratives of the state itself, and these are not confined to political events or legal milestones. If that border is disputed in some way by the state (and, thus, by definition, between at least two states), that narrative becomes complicated further. This complexity and contention are reflected in this chapter, which seeks to explain but a few dimensions of the border by considering its political, economic, security and societal consequences.

Partition

The war in Europe provided an opportunity to a conglomeration of organisations seeking complete Irish independence to organise the Easter Rising of April 1916. This was rapidly suppressed by British armed forces but their subsequent treatment of rebel prisoners (including executions) contributed to growing fervency of nationalist sentiment among the Irish public. The political party Sinn Féin garnered support from across different factions involved in the Rising and became the conduit for the political expression of this sentiment (Garvin, 1981). The conciliatory tactics of Redmond's Irish Parliamentary Party had been seen to fail, and Sinn Féin went to a landslide victory in the general election in 1918. They would not take their seats in Westminster. Instead, Sinn Féin proceeded to declare an

Irish Republic and the first republican parliament (Dáil Éireann) convened in Dublin. At its first meeting, in January 1919, it made a Declaration of Irish Independence, solemnly declaring 'foreign government in Ireland to be an invasion of our national right which we will never tolerate'. The British response was to deem both the Dáil and Sinn Féin illegal. British crown forces (including the notorious Black and Tans) were sent to assist the Royal Irish Constabulary against the Irish Republican Army, and the Irish war of independence began.

Knowing he had to act, the British Prime Minister Lloyd George delegated the drafting of a fourth Home Rule bill for Ireland. While it was not the preferred option of either Irish nationalists or Ulster unionists (the Irish Unionist Alliance, somewhat ironically, split over the issue), partition was considered by the British government to be a compromise alternative to an unmaintainable union. Under these circumstances, Ulster Unionists lobbied to ensure that a future Northern Ireland would encompass six of the counties of Ulster (Antrim, Armagh, Down, Fermanagh, Derry/Londonderry and Tyrone) (Lewis, 2005). These comprised the largest area with a 'decisive Protestant majority in which unionist power could be guaranteed' (Ferriter, 2019: 8). The resulting legislation, the Government of Ireland Act, was approved by the Westminster Parliament and received royal assent in December 1920. It provided for separate parliaments for 'Southern Ireland' and for the six north-eastern counties of 'Northern Ireland', as well as for an all-island Council of Ireland:

> With a view to the eventual establishment of a Parliament for the whole of Ireland, and to bringing about harmonious action between the parliaments and governments of Southern Ireland and Northern Ireland, and to the promotion of mutual intercourse and uniformity in relation to matters affecting the whole of Ireland. (Art. 2.i)

However, while the 40 Unionist of the 52 MPs in the northern parliament seized upon the creation of Northern Ireland, the new legislature in the south was boycotted and then suspended (Coleman, 2014). Home Rule for Dublin was not enough to bring the war of independence to an end. That came with the Anglo-Irish Treaty of 1921, which saw the creation of the Irish Free State, which contained greater powers for the Irish Parliament and Executive than Home Rule. The Irish Free State was in principle envisaged as covering the 32 counties. However, whether Ireland remained partitioned was in the hands of politicians (in both the Commons and the Senate) of Northern Ireland. Article 12 of the Anglo-Irish Treaty gave them the right to opt out from the Irish Free State. This they duly did at the earliest possible opportunity, that is the day after the Irish Free State Constitution came into effect, in December 1922.[3] The foundational document of Northern Ireland was thus to continue to be the Government of Ireland Act.

Article 12 of the Anglo-Irish Treaty also provided for the creation of a Boundary Commission of three persons (appointed by the governments of the UK, Ireland and Northern Ireland) to:

> determine in accordance with the wishes of the inhabitants, so far as may be compatible with economic and geographic conditions, the boundaries between Northern Ireland and the rest of Ireland, and ... the boundary of Northern Ireland shall be such as may be determined by such Commission.

This had alarmed unionists, and the British government had privately assured northern Prime Minister James Craig it would be less significant than nationalists hoped for (Rankin, 2005: 19). Nationalists expected more of the Boundary Commission, not least because of the arbitrary character of the Irish border. It had not been negotiated in any specific geographical detail, nor had its imposition been subject to any democratic process, such as a plebiscite. The adherence of those who wielded the pen to centuries-old county lines meant that a number of towns and their hinterlands were separated; in some instances, villages, farms and even houses were divided by the new border (Leary, 2018). Nevertheless, in part because of the continuing violence and the initial refusal of the Northern Ireland government to appoint a commissioner, the Boundary Commission was not established until 1923 and only began work in 1924 (Murray, 2011). It was small and under-resourced, operating under considerable political pressure as well as public speculation. Given the difference of unionist and nationalist views and expectations of the Commission, it had great difficulty in determining what 'the wishes of the inhabitants' were. In the end, the Commission's recommendations were confined to small transfers of land in both directions from the immediate border area (Laffan, 1983; O'Callaghan, 2000). But even those minor adjustments were never made. The Tripartite Boundary Agreement of December 1925 discarded the Council of Ireland and rejected the Commission's work. The 310-mile

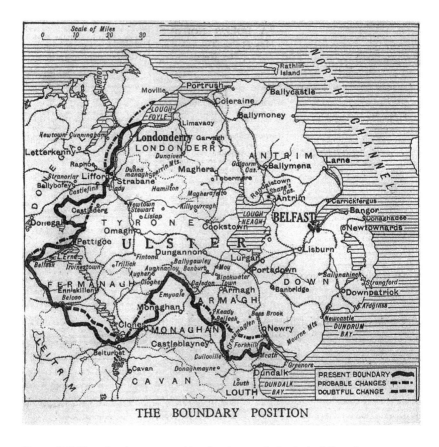

THE BOUNDARY POSITION

Figure 2.2 Map showing proposed border changes in the leaked Boundary Commission report[4]

(499 km) boundary line was left in place. As arbitrary as this borderline was, it was to determine the shape and nature of politics across the island of Ireland for the century to come.

The economic border

From the earliest days of partition, the processes of state-building both north and south gave material effect to the Irish border in a way that would particularly impact upon those living closest to it. Moore's (2019) study demonstrates the extent of the upheaval brought about by partition, including trade, law, services and infrastructure. But there were limits to partition too, not least in the continuation of many all-island organisations, including the main religious denominations. Nevertheless, there had been very real north/south tension even prior to partition. In August 1920, the Sinn Féin-dominated Dáil imposed a boycott on goods and banks from Belfast in protest at discrimination and violence against Catholics in the city. By 1921, this spread as a trade boycott of goods from the north-east. In practice, its greatest impact was on Co. Monaghan, which had close trade, transport and migration ties to Belfast (Dooley, 1994: 90–91). By April 1923, frictions in trade north and south took more concrete form when, in a desperate effort to raise revenue, the Irish Free State began to erect customs posts at border crossing points. At the time of partition, there were around 180 border crossings, only a minority of which became 'approved' crossings on which a motor vehicle could be used (Leary, 2016). The new customs regime was particularly inconvenient for residents in the border region and disruptive to many local retailers (Leary, 2016). It was not merely the cost of the tariffs paid (these were mainly for excise goods such as alcohol, and on some manufactured goods) that caused the difficulties, but the fact of having to use approved routes and make the necessary declarations (Nash et al., 2013). Inevitably, trade across the border diminished almost immediately, and the economy of the part of the island that was now rent in two by the border was badly affected.

The Tripartite Boundary Agreement of December 1925 involved what the Irish Republican newspaper, *An Phoblacht*, described as a deal that saw 'a large section' of the Irish people 'sold into bondage by their coun-trymen' (11 December 1925, cited in Rankin, 2006: 24). In return for rec-ognising the boundary as it had been drawn by the Government of Ireland Act, the Irish Free State was relieved of the liabilities for a share of the UK public debt that it had assumed through the Anglo-Irish Treaty (FitzGerald and Kenny, 2020). However, this did not include the land purchase annui-ties that were included under Article 5. As a consequence, the Irish state continued to collect land annuities from farmers (about 10 per cent of their net income) and pay it into the British land purchase fund. Unsurprisingly, there was strong grassroots resistance to such action from the Irish gov-ernment to service the British economy (Ó Drisceoil, 2011). The cause was taken up by the Fianna Fáil Party, which had been founded by Éamon de

Valera as a breakaway from Sinn Féin after the end of the civil war. When Fianna Fáil came to power in 1932, it withheld the general annuities payment. The British attempted to recoup the loss with a tax on Irish imports; the Irish responded in turn by placing tariffs on British imports. Because (as now) trade policy remained in the remit of Westminster rather than the Northern Ireland Parliament, the harsher customs regime had effect on the Irish border as well as the sea border. This dispute between the Irish and British governments escalated into an Anglo-Irish trade war in 1932, with the most direct impact felt by the border communities, and with knock-on harm to all-island relations. When it came to negotiating the Anglo-Irish Free Trade Agreement of 1938:

> Britain urged the Irish Free State to accord special trading concessions to Northern Ireland both as a gesture of conciliation and to stem protests [from Northern Ireland politicians]. However de Valera argued that such a concession would give Northern Ireland the 'best of both worlds' – partition plus a favourable opportunity of expanding its trade in Eire, opening the floodgates to intrusive competition. (Daly, 1992: 162)

In the end, no concessions were made for Northern Ireland in the treaty.

The Second World War further tested the Irish and British willingness to compromise state interests for Northern Ireland. Documentary evidence suggests that in June 1940, in an effort to persuade Ireland to join forces, the British promised to establish a joint body to deal with the constitutional detail of unity and the possibility of merging the administrations (Longford and O'Neill, 1970). However, de Valera was wise to be sceptical. The Northern Ireland Prime Minister Craig had not been consulted about the matter in advance. The region was also to suffer a public ignominy in the British government's suspension of the Common Travel Area. The Home Office had been reluctant to see passport controls in operation between the United Kingdom and the newly established Irish Free State, believing them unnecessary and cumbersome to enforce across the new sea and land borders. Although formalised only through scattered law rather than legal treaty, the two sides agreed to enforce each other's immigration rules for 'aliens' and to treat British and Irish citizens as non-alien, requiring no leave to enter or to stay in their respective territories (Ryan, 2001: 856). During the War (until 1952), the British imposed passport checks on all people entering Great Britain from the island of Ireland, on the grounds that invasion of either island was a real threat (Butler and Barrett, 2018: 283; Delaney, 2001: 50). On that occasion, and in the context of tumult in European relations, the relative ease of managing movement across the Irish Sea (compared with monitoring entry into Northern Ireland from the Irish Free State) provoked a pragmatic approach at border management from British authorities – even in the face of unionist ire.

The violent border

The Government of Ireland Act (1920) and the Anglo-Irish Treaty (1921) were drawn in the context of the war of independence in Ireland, at a time when it seemed 'increasingly beyond the control of Britain's civilian and military authorities' (Costello, 1988: 8). Violence in the north was primarily in Belfast, and often followed a pattern in which Irish Republican Army (IRA) attacks on security forces were then avenged by loyalist attacks on Catholics. The British government announced the formation of the Ulster Special Constabulary of armed volunteers in November 1920, to support the work of the police and army in tackling the IRA. Recruitment to the force, especially for the part-time B Specials, was rapid, drawing on Protestant fears of nationalist insurgency as well as a number of pre-existing militia or vigilante groups, including the Ulster Volunteer Force. In 1922, the Specials took to 'securing' the border by putting fortified checkpoints on main crossing points and making some secondary roads impassable. The IRA response to this was predictable. What was damaged the most, of course, were the conditions for daily life among residents of communities which now happened to be riven by the border.

> Farmers will not till the land. There is no trade across the border … Men who lived with each other in perfect harmony and ridiculed the idea of the border now see what partition has brought about. (Anglo-Celt newspaper [Cavan and Monaghan], 18 March 1922, quoted in Dorney, 2019)

The coherence of the IRA's border strategy withered as the civil war began. Over the course of the century, whether the border was a violent one or not depended in the first instance on the IRA, its strategy and its actions. The decades after the civil war were a period of internal division and diminishment for the IRA. Thirty years later, its first sustained campaign was to focus on the Irish border as a symbolic and material manifestation of British rule in Ireland. The campaign began in late 1956. Its targets included BBC transmitters, a courthouse, B Specials posts, Royal Ulster Constabulary (RUC) barracks and customs posts. The reaction from the Irish state, under a Fianna Fáil government, was harsh, including internment (imprisonment without trial) for IRA volunteers. But the clearest reason for the campaign's failure was the lack of public support for its activities, specifically nationalist indifference (Moloney, 2007). Calling the already-collapsed campaign to an official end in 1962, the IRA statement called 'for increased support' as it entered a period of 'consolidation'. No one anticipated the dramatic and spiralling violence that was to emerge within the decade.

Civil rights protests in the late 1960s were responded to with brutality by the RUC, particularly in Derry city. By August 1969, the situation was so perilous that Taoiseach Jack Lynch called for the deployment of a United Nations peacekeeping force to Northern Ireland, and the Irish Army established field hospitals and refugee camps at the border (Fanning, 2001). The British government also turned to the military, but in a more direct way. While initially intended to restore order, the actions of British soldiers in Northern Ireland further inflamed tensions. Paramilitary forces re-emerged among communities, using tactics of terror, intimidation and savage sectarianism. As the Troubles escalated, unionists urged action from state authorities to secure the border, believing violence (not without some justification) to be increasing as a result of incursion into Northern Ireland from republicans based in the south (Patterson, 2013). In response, the British Army would 'crater' or 'spike' roads, including minor roads that were seen as obvious routes into the north for those with nefarious intentions. Locals would then refill the craters or remove the spikes, angry at the inconvenience caused to their daily lives by these road blocks, as well as at the demonstration of British state power. This process of closing and reopening roads would happen dozens of times in places, until the British Army then moved to close roads on a more permanent basis. But – far from removing the terrorist threat – such road closures led to an increase in violent incidences at the border (Mulroe, 2017: 91). The border was also a barometer for republican reactions to security policy within Northern Ireland. Before the government's policy of internment was enacted by the British Army in August 1971, there were on average four border 'incidents' a month. This rose to 16 a month after internment, and to 33 per month after 'cratering' (Mulroe, 2017: 91). We see in this process the way in which the border is a micro-level manifestation of wider tensions, even tensions between the two governments. Again, the worst effects of this are felt by border communities.

Rosemary Harris's (1972) social anthropological study of a border community was originally conducted in the early 1950s, 20 years before it was published. It revealed the depths of sectarianism that existed alongside mundane (necessary) habits of interaction in a small border village. Being published when it was, it went some way towards explaining the background context for the neighbour-upon-neighbour suspicion and violence that emerged around some parts of the border during the Troubles. One local resident explained the particularly sinister effects of conflict in the border region:

> Border communities are remote and were very much left to themselves. They were also easy pickings in the Troubles. Very many communities were very isolated. They were easily targeted homes and houses and individuals. And it was very much a neighbour on neighbour conflict, so it was very personal … When it came to rural regions, they had to work out who was going to be killed and how and where and when and that very often meant neighbour spying on neighbour and that is a deep level of mistrust and hurt and has a legacy … It happened on both sides of the community. (Interview with the author, November 2020)

Colm Tóibín's (1987) *Walking along the Border* was perhaps the first to attempt to describe the uniqueness of the border region: the visible presence and effects of conflict mingled with the low-key familiarity and canny pragmatism of the locals. Following in his footsteps 30 years later, Garret Carr (2017) describes the borderland as being a realm of its own. Geology, folklore, religious practices, ghost stories and the tragedies of 'the disappeared' come together in his description of a place and people encapsulating liminality. Such books on 'the border' itself remain relatively rare – perhaps because of a lingering wariness of even inadvertently reifying it, even after a hundred years of its existence. Studies of partition are more common. Historiographical interventions on the subject mirror the concerns of their generation and are thus illuminating in their own way. Such studies have predominantly come from Irish scholars; what these works contain, assume and elucidate are in their own way emblematic of Ireland's process of nation-state building and, inexorably, its relationship with Britain (O'Callaghan, 2006).

Situating analyses of partition

The first 'wave' of books on the topic of partition came about 20 years after partition itself, in the wake of the 'Emergency' and around the time of the Republic of Ireland Act in 1948 (Healy, 1945; O'Neill, 1946). The All-Party Anti-Partition Conference (1950) was established at this time too, on the initiative of Seán McBride, the Minister for External Affairs in the new coalition government (Coakley, 2017: 4). Its statement on 'Ireland's right to unity' (1950) was an effort to formalise and disseminate an irredentist policy (in its claim over the territory of another state), but now informed by what it sardonically referred to as 'the new "democracy"' in Northern Ireland. With all the main parties in the south participating, the 'unity' that this initiative served was primarily one of a shared official narrative in the new Republic of Ireland vis-à-vis Northern Ireland. In sum, it claimed, partition was an historical, political and cultural aberration, and the harm of British colonial interference could only be undone by the full independence of the island of Ireland as one nation-state.

The next 'wave' of texts on partition came in the early 1980s. Prominent among these were the contributions of historians such as Michael Laffan (1983), Nicholas Mansergh (1978) and Tom Fraser (1984), who sought to understand the partition of Ireland in its international context. But one of the most notable contributions came from Clare O'Halloran (1987), in a book originally based on a masters' thesis. She argued that, while irredentist rhetoric may have been commonplace in official discourse, the effects of the policies of the Irish state were cumulatively to reinforce partition. O'Halloran's critique included the contemporary New Ireland Forum, which was established in 1983 by the Taoiseach Garret FitzGerald to identify, through dialogue, potential alternative political arrangements to those currently in place for Northern Ireland. She excoriates the 'inherent self-deception of nationalist thinking' present in the Forum report's claim that a united Ireland 'would restore the historic integrity of Ireland and end the divisions in the country'. Such divisions, O'Halloran remarked, 'have long centred on the very question of unity and continue to do so' (1987: 209).

The fact that a majority vote in England and Wales for leaving the EU in the June 2016 referendum spurred a further wave of books on the topic of partition is another sign of the unique circumstances on the island of Ireland. Common to these studies is an attempt to understand the degree to which Ireland was internally divided, while at the same time identifying the lack of justification for the creation of the Irish border. Lynch (2019) notes that the 'two nation view of Ireland' pre-dated partition but is keen to reject any notion that it was anyway inevitable that the Irish Question would become the 'Ulster Question'. He highlights the 'chaotic, confused' character of partition. This point is also reflected in Rast's (2019: 14) study, which explores the 'manifold contingencies that contributed to the settlement that emerged in 1922'. His analysis has much contemporary resonance: 'Decisions were made for specific reasons, some ideological, others political, and still others because the decision-makers believed they had no viable alternative' (Rast, 2019: 17). Rast makes a particularly strong argument that much difficulty in the years up to 1925 was caused by the discrepancy between what leaders privately thought and what they shared in public. The temptation to use rhetoric to distract from real harms or problematic decisions is particularly strong in a context of political flux, but it also holds particular dangers at such times.

The first chapter of Diarmaid Ferriter's *The Border* (2019) is titled 'The long gestation', and reflects an effort to be sensitive to unionist sensibilities:

> Ideological partition was long a reality in Ireland before the physical border was imposed, owing to the distinctive development of Ulster. (Ferriter, 2019: 1)

His claim is reminiscent of that in one of the most heterodox books on the Irish border, that by the Dutch geographer Marcus Heslinga. Originally published in 1971, Heslinga argues that the border marks a pre-existing 'cultural divide'. Changing the 'map' from a focus on the territory of the island to the 'British Isles', he identifies regions that cross the Irish Sea in an effort to explain differences within Ireland. A more nuanced approach to the subject of 'the border' was taken three decades later. This time an interdisciplinary approach allowed for consideration of landscape and literature, as well as history and politics (Anderson and Bort, 1999). While wary of implying any determinism behind the border, contributors to the volume identify structural and political differences between north and south prior to partition, as well as ones that have grown as a consequence of it. Ferriter's (2019) characterisation of the border is in this vein. While being explicit that 'British duplicity' is responsible for the creation of the Irish border, he also argues that Irish republicans played their part in deepening the effects of partition. Ultimately, he sees Northern Ireland as the product of Anglo-Irish politics and failures of diplomacy, and the Irish border itself as the site of some of the worst such decisions. Ferriter sees Brexit in this vein. He regrets that what he refers to as 'the weight of Anglo-Irish history' embodied in the Irish border made so little impression on those who championed the UK's withdrawal from the EU. As a consequence, the Brexit process itself became afflicted by the tendency of 'the Irish border' to 'polarise and frustrate, with reverberations well beyond Britain and Ireland' (Ferriter, 2019: 144). We will explore the reasons for this 'tendency', and the nature of those reverberations, in the next chapter.

Notes

1. This map was drawn by Sarah Gearty (after J. H. Whyte, *New History of Ireland*) and was originally published in *History Ireland* (see Walker, 2005). It is reproduced here with their kind permission.
2. By 1914, a British Covenant in support apparently garnered around 2 million signatures. Rather than opposing the principle of Home Rule for Ireland, it was mobilised to oppose 'the people of Ulster' being denied 'their rights as citizens of the United Kingdom' (Parkinson, 2012).
3. The phrasing of Article 12 in the Anglo-Irish Treaty which allowed for this has been subject to much historical analysis: 'If ... an address is presented to His Majesty by both Houses of the Parliament of Northern Ireland to that effect, the powers of the Parliament and Government of the Irish Free State shall no longer extend to Northern Ireland, and the provisions of the Government of Ireland Act, 1920, (including those relating to the Council of Ireland) shall, so far as they relate to Northern Ireland, continue to be of full force and effect.'
4. This map was published as part of a leak on the draft report of the Boundary Commission to the *Morning Post* newspaper (7 November 1925). It is reproduced here with the kind permission of the Deputy Keeper of the Public Records Office of Northern Ireland (reference D3015/3/B/2).

what do we know?

EU membership created the conditions for a more open Irish border

When the United Kingdom first applied for membership of the European Economic Community (EEC) in 1961, Ireland had little choice but to do so also. And the process of Ireland's application for membership was affected (read delayed) by the EEC's (read de Gaulle's) view of the UK. Many historical analyses posit that Ireland's application for EEC membership went alongside that of the UK's because it was then still economically dependent on its neighbour, even after decades of independence. However, it is important not to ignore the presence of the Irish border in this calculation. If the UK was to be part of the EEC without Ireland, then the Irish border would become even more of a barrier to trade and cooperation than it already was. The argument made by the Irish government for membership was not about avoiding hardening the Irish border but about making it less significant. In the campaign for a Yes vote in the 1972 referendum on Ireland's accession to the EEC, the Department of Foreign Affairs issued a pamphlet which argued that EEC membership would remove tariffs and 'other restrictions on trade between the two parts of the country' (DFA, 1972: 1). Cross-border movement of people would also increase, it predicted, as EEC membership would lift restrictions on people from the Republic gaining employment in Northern Ireland. It also claimed that both north and south would be subject to the same policies on 'matters of great importance', including the Common Agricultural Policy. Nevertheless, as significant as it would be to have the island of Ireland part of the wider Common Market, the Irish government was clear that this would not automatically produce closer relationships across the border. Taoiseach Jack Lynch spelled this out in a speech delivered to an audience in Dundalk, a border town, a year before the referendum on accession:

> Continental entrepreneurs will not be concerned with political borders or outmoded political attitudes in this country. And the Governments of the Common Market countries will not be interested either. It is Irish people who must diminish the differences between us in step with the dismantlement of tariff walls. It is we who must concert our actions and promote our common interests. (Lynch, 1971)

But – as Leave voters are well aware – European integration is about far more than trade and investment. The movement of services and people across the EU has expanded beyond the principle of non-discrimination. Protections for frontier workers developed in the EU were particularly beneficial for those living on one side of the Irish border and working on the other. The same is true of the Treatment Abroad scheme, which enabled people to receive healthcare on the other side of the border if not otherwise available to them. The UK and Ireland actively engaged in EU-funded schemes for cooperation between education and research bodies. The sharing of information between police services across the EU, and the development of criminal justice cooperation mechanisms such as the European Arrest Warrant, also enhanced the conditions for security on the island of Ireland and across the Common Travel Area more broadly (Davies, 2020). Above all else, the context of the EU allowed cross-border cooperation and movement to become depoliticised and normalised. The significance of this is hard to overstate, coming as it did after so many decades of tension and drift.

After accession in 1973, the ending of customs duties and quotas on movement of goods between the UK and Ireland (with some exceptions, e.g. excise goods) reduced the impact of crossing the border. The simplification of customs and transit procedures by the EEC in 1987 further eased the transportation of goods across the island and between Great Britain and Ireland. The creation of the Single Market, when the Treaty on European Union came into effect on 1 January 1993, erased many obstacles to the free movement of goods across the Irish border (and Irish Sea).

Figure 3.1 Advert from Fianna Fáil before the 1972 referendum on accession to the EEC[1]

The process of creating the EU internal market, including harmonising regulatory systems and indirect taxation, has further reduced trade friction across borders within the EU. Added to this, the European Community created and funded programmes in the border region. In 1983, the Economic and Social Committee of the EEC produced a study of 'Irish border areas' to recommend investment from the European Regional Development Fund. It noted that 'in many parts' essential infrastructure and water supply were 'clearly inadequate and those which do exist are sometimes disrupted by damage caused by troubles in the area' (ECOSOC, 1983: 1). Notably, this was its one reference to the context of the Troubles, so sensitive was the subject for British–Irish relations at the time. Overall, the report offers a rather sombre analysis of a woefully-underdeveloped region. Over the decades to come, EU investment in the area and cross-border infrastructure was typical of its wider cross-border cooperation policy, as well as a core element of its support for the peace process (Buchanan, 2014; Harguindéguy and Hayward, 2014).

Relations between 'these islands' are interwoven and interdependent

Michael Kennedy's (2000) archival work reveals that cross-border activity prior to EEC accession had been carried out with great caution and often in secrecy. He notes that the ambitions for cross-border projects were often quite grand, but their success was limited and depended largely on being able to keep them 'out of politics'. The public meetings of the Northern Ireland Prime Minister Terence O'Neill with Taoisigh (first Sean Lemass, then Jack Lynch) in the mid-1960s may have been significant in themselves, but they also brought new risks to such cooperation. As the civil rights movement gathered pace in 1968, the very act of meeting together was more likely to be seen as treasonous than sensible by those whom O'Neill and Lynch were trying to lead. Cross-border cooperation became more difficult, and more hidden. In light of this, the ambition of the Sunningdale Agreement (1973) is all the more remarkable. Within a year of accession to the EEC, the two governments proposed an all-island Council of Ireland. This 'would undertake important work relating, for instance, to the impact of EEC membership', in light of the Council's 'harmonizing functions'. Although that initiative was to prove ill-fated, the importance of the EEC as the context for agreement between the two governments and for cross-border cooperation only grew. This was acknowledged in the preamble to the Anglo-Irish Agreement (1985), which was to be repeated in the 1998 British–Irish Agreement:

> Wishing further to develop the unique relationship between their peoples and the close co-operation between their countries as friendly neighbours and as partners in the European Community.

The Anglo-Irish Agreement formalised an 'Irish dimension' to the governance of Northern Ireland. An intergovernmental conference was established for 'consultation' between the British and Irish governments, mainly on security matters but also with a remit to promote cross-border cooperation. Most controversially, the Agreement established a 'permanent' presence for Irish officials in Northern Ireland, in the form of a secretariat based in Maryfield, just outside Belfast. One of the first officials there for the Department for Foreign Affairs, Dáithí O'Ceallaigh (2019: 88–89), described what was entailed in the 100-mile (160 km) journey from Dublin to Belfast in those days:

> We initially travelled in military aircraft, with the Aer Corps from Baldonnel to Aldergrove military airport and from there to Maryfield in British army helicopters, later in RUC vehicles … One of my abiding memories is going in on the initial flight on 8 December 1985; it was a historic moment. We represented the presence, for the first time since partition in 1921, of the Irish government within Northern Ireland, within the United Kingdom to deal with Northern Ireland affairs: it was unique … On the other hand, I was actually quite scared.

He had reason to be apprehensive. There was a standing protest outside the Maryfield 'bunker'. Unionist reaction to the Anglo-Irish Agreement had been vehement and visible, including a 400,000 signature petition and huge rallies. Rev. Ian Paisley (24 November 1985) addressed a huge crowd in Belfast city centre, not sparing either government from his wrath:

> Where do the terrorists operate from? From the Irish Republic! That's where they come from! Where do the terrorists return to for sanctuary? To the Irish Republic! And yet Mrs Thatcher tells us that that Republic must have some say in our Province. We say never, never, never, never!

This time loyalist protestations proved unable to shift the British government's commitment to the inclusion of an 'Irish dimension' in the governance of Northern Ireland. The Downing Street Declaration (1993), which preceded the Framework Documents (1995) and the multiparty talks leading to the 1998 Agreement, set out the need for 'a new political framework' that would encompass 'arrangements within Northern Ireland, for the whole island, and between these islands'. In these terms, the conflict was not seen as confined to or by the matter of partition. As such, its resolution would also need to be about more than partition; it should be about 'relationships between the peoples of both islands'. The integral connections between British–Irish and north/south relationships are formalised in the 1998 Agreement.

The 1998 Agreement transformed cross-border relations, east/west and north/south

The 1998 Agreement comprises two documents: a multiparty agreement by most of Northern Ireland's political parties and an international agreement between the British and Irish governments to implement and underpin what the parties agreed. The parties to the Agreement affirmed their commitment 'to the mutual respect, the civil rights, and the religious liberties of everyone in the community'; this included 'the right to seek constitutional change by peaceful and legitimate means'. It introduced a statutory obligation to promote 'parity of esteem between the two main communities', monitored by the Equality Commission. It is noteworthy that policies for sustained economic growth and stability are incorporated under the heading of 'Rights, Safeguards and Equality of Opportunity'. The connection between economic prosperity and tackling division is evident in the proposition for a regional development strategy 'tackling the problems of a divided society and social cohesion in urban, rural and border areas'. In the Agreement, economic, social and cultural issues are seen as intrinsically linked.

Also interlocking and interdependent are the institutional and constitutional arrangements provided for in the Agreement. At its core (Strand One) is the Northern Ireland Assembly, the prime source of authority in respect of all devolved responsibilities. For external relationships, the First Minister and deputy First Minister share the duty of coordinating 'the response of the Northern Ireland administration to external relationships'.

But there is something very particular about the north/south relationship (Strand Two). The Agreement states that the success of the Assembly and the North/South Ministerial Council (NSMC) 'depends on that of the other'. Through the NSMC, ministers from Ireland and Northern Ireland are responsible for areas designated for cross-border cooperation, and there are dedicated teams for this in each civil service department affected (Tannam, 2006: 12). According to the 1998 Agreement, the NSMC functions to exchange information and 'to develop consultation, cooperation and action within the island of Ireland'. The goal is to 'reach agreement on the adoption of common policies' where relevant, or alternatively to decide on policies for separate implementation. This includes, the 1998 Agreement continues, through 'implementation on an all-island and cross-border basis' on 'matters of mutual interest' within the competence of the NI Executive and Irish Government.[2] Either the Northern Ireland Executive or the Irish government can propose any matter for consideration or action by the NSMC. Powers with legislative authority have been transferred from the governments to the north/south implementation bodies, including the Special EU Programmes Body, InterTrade Ireland, Waterways Ireland and SafeFood.[3] Thus, the Agreement provides for institutions that have competence to operate on an all-island basis.[4] In addition, the Agreement identified 12 areas for cooperation between the two jurisdictions. Such areas include agriculture (including animal and plant health), education (e.g. teacher qualifications and exchanges), transport (e.g. cross-rail service), environment (e.g. water quality, waste management), social security (e.g. entitlements of cross-border workers and fraud control) and health (e.g. emergency ambulance transfers). The UK–EU 'mapping exercise' conducted in 2017 identified around 150 examples of such ongoing cross-border cooperation, about two-thirds of which was directly or indirectly enabled by common EU membership and underpinned by EU law (EC & HMG, 2019a).

But north/south cooperation has not been merely a local affair. The British–Irish relationship has enabled it, and not just at the intergovernmental level. Coakley et al. (2005) explain that constitutional reform across the UK in the late 1990s was critically important for post-Agreement territorial innovation on the island of Ireland. Devolved legislative and executive decision-making and policy-setting powers in Scotland, Wales and Northern Ireland not only meant adjustment to intra-UK relations, but also meant potential new developments for British–Irish relations more broadly.

The Strand Three bodies of the 1998 Agreement should be seen in this light. The British–Irish Intergovernmental Conference (BIIGC) was intended to be the forum for 'regular and frequent meetings' regarding non-devolved matters. In a step considerably beyond that of the Irish dimension acco-modated by the 1985 Anglo-Irish Agreement, the BIIGC allows the Irish government to 'put forward views and proposals'. This is, according to the 1998 Agreement, in 'recognition of the Irish Government's special interest in Northern Ireland and of the extent to which issues of mutual concern arise in relation to Northern Ireland'. A much broader body is the British–Irish Council (BIC), which serves to 'promote the harmonious and mutually beneficial development of the totality of relationships among the peoples of these islands'. It incorporates the British and Irish governments, the executives/governments of the devolved nations and regions, plus repre-sentatives of the Isle of Man and Channel Islands. The BIC remit is simi-lar to the NSMC but working on an east/west basis, on such matters as transport, environment, agriculture and 'approaches to EU issues'. It was envisaged that the BIC would produce 'practical cooperation on agreed policies'. However, Coakley and Laffan (2005: 221) presciently argued that the success of these east/west and north/south bodies depended on two processes that were beyond their ability to control. The first is that of Euro-pean integration, the context of which was so important in enabling such cross-border innovation in the first place. The second, 'more subtle force' they identified was, 'the legacy of history, and of the past imperial-type rela-tionship between the two islands' (Coakley and Laffan, 2005: 221). Brexit has revealed the susceptibility of the former and the tenacity of the latter.

Cross-border cooperation is susceptible to political circumstances

In 1995, Dominic Murray conducted a survey of cross-border links on the island. He later (1999: 211) reflected on the 'reticence' of Northern Ireland bodies to promote their cross-border links publicly 'because of the pos-sible "political baggage" that might be attributed to them'. A few years later, a wholly 'new climate' for cross-border activity had been created by the Good Friday (Belfast) Agreement. The Centre for Cross Border Stud-ies established in Armagh in 1999, under the directorship of Andy Pollak, embodied the sense that the Agreement – in a way quite removed from political aspirations – created new opportunities for connectivity across the island. The Mapping Frontiers, Plotting Pathways project, funded through the Irish Higher Education Authority, was an academic response to the belief that 'the significance of the border has changed' and been 'redefined' through the 1998 Agreement (Coakley and O'Dowd, 2007: 24). In and of itself, however, the treaty did not set cross-border cooperation on an inexorable course. Interdisciplinary analysis of post-Agreement institutional, policy, civil society and administrative cooperation often returned to doubts regarding its sustainability (Byrne et al., 2009; Hayward, 2007; O'Dowd et al., 2006). These were exacerbated by the collapse of the Assembly and the return to a period of direct rule from Westminster for nearly five years. As it turned out, the 'golden age' for cross-border cooperation was rather short-lived.

Post-1998 Agreement optimism coincided with the economic boom in the Republic of Ireland. The economists John Bradley and Esmond Birnie (2001) wondered whether the Celtic Tiger could 'cross the Irish border'. In practice, the north was but barely hit by the tail of the tiger on its way out. The restoration of the Executive in 2007, following the St Andrews Agreement that brought the DUP and Sinn Féin into power-sharing, happened just before the global financial crisis which had such a devastating impact south of the border. After a decade as one of the fastest growing economies in Europe, Ireland suffered the humiliation of being dependent on a bailout from the International Monetary Fund (IMF) and European Financial Stability Fund, including a contribution from its nearest neighbour. The shock was severe. There was no spare money for Ireland's infrastructure or public services. Despite the ambition of the coordinated development plans between Northern Ireland and the Republic, economic priorities returned to focus either side of the border.

In the wake of the crisis, cross-border initiatives seemed more of a luxury than a necessity. The most high-profile achievements for cross-border cooperation in the ensuing period were the product of many years of careful planning, and the leadership of determined individuals, such as the North West Cancer Centre funded by both the Irish government and Northern Ireland Executive and providing treatment for patients across the border region. And, quietly too, there were other initiatives by individuals in various sectors – voluntary groups, the police services, local authorities, teachers, businesses – that established low-key habits of cooperation for the benefit of local residents. Indeed, it is no exaggeration to say that many people in the region live cross-border lives. This was illustrated by one woman living in Donegal (Republic of Ireland) who described what the open border meant for her:

> I work in Derry. My children are educated in Donegal. When they go to third level, institutions in NI [Northern Ireland] would be my first choice. I access healthcare in ROI [Republic of Ireland] for convenience, but if I needed care at a specialist level I would opt to use services in NI due to the distance to access services in Galway or Dublin. Derry is our city and economic hub … The social links are very strong. The opening of the roads which were closed to us for years meant so much to our communities. As family, we shop, travel, engage in leisure in NI. (Survey respondent quoted in Hayward, 2018: 32)

Such connections were aided by the conditions of European integration but they were attributed to the difference made by the 1998 Agreement and what that meant for British–Irish and north/south relations (Hayward, 2017). In this way, the open border was totemic of the peace process. But border communities are particularly vulnerable to decisions made at the centres of power. The prospect of Brexit and the transformation of the Irish border into an external border of the EU induced a profound sense of fear and uncertainty among those in the border region. This was not only because of its implications in practical terms, but also because of wider ramifications for the British–Irish and north/south relationship:

> My family live, work, study, socialise and shop both sides of the border every single day. We cannot plan ahead re: work or study opportunities due to Brexit uncertainty. We live in a town severely impacted by the conflict and there is a real sense the return to borders will raise tensions and lead to the Good Friday Agreement being undermined. (Survey respondent from the central border region, cited in Hayward, 2018: 27)

Ó Beacháin (2019) explains that the risk posed by Brexit for the peace process is because it changes the British–Irish relationship. Their partnership in the EU created the conditions in which a joint approach to Northern Ireland could be forged and sustained. The Brexit vote demonstrated how exposed the 1998 Agreement is to the asymmetry of the British–Irish relationship, regardless of the expressed wishes of a majority of people in Northern Ireland. This environment has been greatly complicated by the Protocol on Ireland/Northern Ireland in the UK–EU Withdrawal Agreement.

The British–Irish relationship is now itself vulnerable to the asymmetry of the UK–EU relationship. On 29 January 2021, to the shock and consternation of both the British and Irish governments, the European Commission proposed to activate safeguard measures under Article 16 of the Protocol to ban the movement of the scarce resource of the coronavirus vaccine across the Irish border into Northern Ireland. Although the Commission quickly retreated – describing the matter as a 'misjudgement' – the fact that it happened at all was viewed by the DUP as 'both revealing and a very significant game-changer' (DUP, 2021). The party sought to unite unionists in a campaign to 'Free us from Protocol'. In order to underline their opposition, the party stated its intention: 'to send a strong signal to the Government of the Republic of Ireland that North-South relationships are also impacted' (DUP, 2021). The withholding of engagement in north/south bodies is a well-established form of unionist protest. The hardline Traditional Unionist Voice party welcomed the DUP's tactic: 'We continue to believe that the greatest political leverage lies in discomforting north/southery' (TUV, 2021). This sentiment was echoed by former First Minister Peter Robinson (2021), who remarked: 'One lesson learned after decades of dealing with governments is that they don't yield unless life has become uncomfortable.' However, the reality of the situation is that now they need to persuade not just Dublin or London of their concerns, but the EU Commission and remaining 27 EU member-states. The ability of any groups in Northern Ireland to cause any discomfort to the decision-makers is sorely limited.

Brexit has reignited the 'border question'

The very first article and section of the Northern Ireland Act (1998), which put the 1998 Agreement into UK law, allows that a referendum in the region could change the constitutional status of Northern Ireland and, thus, the constitution of the United Kingdom – not to mention that of Ireland. The Secretary of State of Northern Ireland has held discretionary power to call a referendum on Irish unification since 1973. This power followed the 'border poll' that took place on 8 March 1973 as part of the British government's somewhat misguided 'hope of taking the Border out of the day-to-day political scene' (Hansard, 1972: 1859). When asked whether such a poll would be 'consultative only', and not in substitution for the provision of the Ireland Act (1949) (which required the consent of the Northern Ireland

Parliament 'for any change in the Border'), Prime Minister Edward Heath elaborated:

> Although Northern Ireland may be separated geographically ... we have always been insistent, and so far the people of Northern Ireland have always been insistent, that they are part of the United Kingdom, equal in every way to the other parts of the United Kingdom. In our view this remains the case until, if it should happen at some future time, a majority decide that they wish the position to be otherwise. What we are doing is to create both an assurance and an opportunity, through the plebiscite, to confirm that that position will be held. (Hansard, 1972: 1868)

Although Heath allows that the principle of majority consent here could ultimately see a united Ireland come to pass, it is clear that the intention behind the use of the referendum then was to bolster the union. Nationalists boycotted the March 1973 poll, under the leadership of the newly formed Social Democratic and Labour Party (SDLP). There was a 99 per cent vote for Northern Ireland to remain in the UK, on a turnout of 58 per cent (WGURII, 2020). Although there has not been such a referendum since, there have been calls for it, both consistently from Sinn Féin and, occasionally, from unionists wishing to call republicans' 'bluff'.[5] Since mid-2016, there has been no such bluff-calling. Indeed, a few unionist politicians have cautiously warned of the need 'to advance the cause of the union' in sensible preparation for a potential referendum on Irish unification (Breen, 2021; Robinson, 2021a). Speculation about – and even anticipation of – a 'border poll' has become commonplace in political and media commentary far beyond the island of Ireland.[6]

A few weeks after the Brexit referendum, Taoiseach Enda Kenny stated his opinion that the UK–EU negotiations should bear in mind that the 1998 Agreement allows for a referendum on Irish unification (Kenny, 2016). Earlier that same day, on his first visit to the region as Secretary of State, James Brokenshire (2016) had ruled out holding any such referendum, commenting that it was 'difficult to see how' Northern Ireland could remain in the EU. Nevertheless, the very potential – and implications of – a referendum on Irish unification had been given entirely new significance by Brexit. At the same European Council meeting that approved the guidelines for Article 50 negotiations, Kenny successfully persuaded his fellow EU leaders to agree a declaration on Ireland in the 'statement for the minutes'. This guaranteed that, in the eventuality of Irish unification, Northern Ireland would automatically rejoin the EU (Staunton and Leahy, 2017). This did not feel like a mere political gesture but a wise move. Richard Humphreys (2018), a judge in the Irish High Court, saw the 'seismic constitutional' event of Brexit as bringing into sharper focus the provisions in the 1998 Agreement for a smoother constitutional transition towards a united Ireland.

By the time the Irish border became centre stage in the withdrawal negotiations, it was already a live subject for discussion among the residents of Ireland, north and south. What the *Northern Ireland Life and Times* (NILT) surveys of social attitudes since mid-2016 show is that there has not been a significant growth in the proportion of Catholic respondents describing themselves as 'nationalist'.[7] But we have seen the proportion of Catholics saying that the long-term policy for Northern Ireland should be for it 'to reunify with the rest of Ireland' increase significantly (32 per cent in 2015, 47 per cent in 2019). We have also seen a significant strengthening of that nationalist identity. In 2016, 18 per cent of nationalists said that they would consider themselves to be 'very strongly' nationalist; this had risen to 31 per cent in 2019. Unionist identity also strengthened in this time, but less dramatically (from 17 per cent 'very strongly' unionist in 2016, to 26 per cent in 2019). Notably, however, these strong unionist and nationalist identities pale into insignificance against the strength of 'Remain' and 'Leave' identities. While the majority of respondents say that they are neither unionist nor nationalist, only a quarter of respondents say that they do not think of themselves as either a Remainer or a Leaver. What is more, these Brexit-related identities are very strongly held: 58 per cent of Remainers consider themselves 'very strong' Remainers, and 54 per cent of Leavers hold that Leave identity 'very strongly'. So Brexit is a highly pertinent political divide in Northern Ireland, although not one that falls equally down the 'communal divide'. Unionists are much more divided than nationalists on this matter; while the latter are predominantly pro-Remain, around a quarter of unionists are pro-Remain and half are pro-Leave (NILT, 2019). However, there is a communal difference when it comes to how people assess the impact of Brexit on Irish unity. Unsurprisingly, there is a communal difference in these responses, with nationalists increasingly in favour of Irish unification and increasingly expectant of it as a result of Brexit.

Speaking in a focus group convened in the border region a few months before the UK left the EU, one local resident explained how the question of a border poll had risen up the agenda since Brexit:

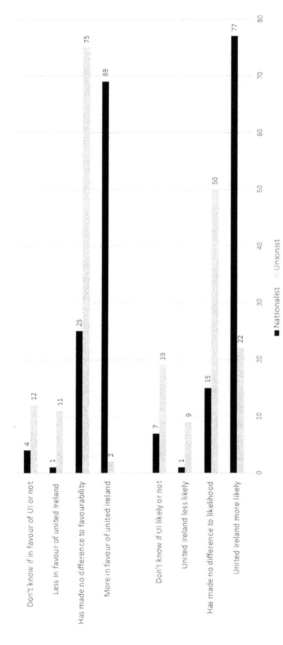

Figure 3.2 Does Brexit make a united Ireland (UI) more likely … and does it make you more in favour of a united Ireland?

Source: NI Life and Times Survey (NILT), 2019

> There were a lot of people in the nationalist and republican commu-
> nity that were happy enough – a border poll might come in 40 years
> … – that's gone. I've heard from people who now saying our future
> lies on the island of Ireland, with all of the people …That is now an
> everyday conversation with people that I'm meeting. It wasn't before
> Brexit … people are now saying there's only one solution to this
> whole issue; we want back into Europe. (Hayward and Komarova,
> 2019: 38–39)

Cochrane (2020) argues that the very existence of Northern Ireland has
been jeopardised by Brexit. In so doing, he points not only to a possible
referendum on Irish unity but also to the destabilising effect of violent conflict from either republicans or loyalists. Just six weeks after the end of the
Brexit transition period, a former DUP First Minister saw fit to warn that
loyalists might take such a path:

> Lurking in the background is the potential for violence stirred up by
> opposition to the Protocol. Such an outbreak linked to a campaign to
> ditch the Protocol would be hugely damaging. Yet history shows, and
> it is my experience, that unionist leaders have had little success in
> controlling those who may opt for such activity. (Peter Robinson,
> 2021)

And the cause of this threat, Robinson claims, is 'the border in the Irish
Sea' that 'politicians from the Republic' and 'their EU mates imposed'. The
UK government did not rush to correct this impression; nor did it endeavour to explain the reasons behind the Protocol it agreed with the EU and is
jointly responsible for implementing.

'Avoiding a hard border' contradicted the logic of Brexit

When the British Prime Minister, Theresa May, wrote to the President of the
EU Council, Donald Tusk, to trigger Article 50 of the Treaty on European
Union and set the clock ticking on the UK's exit from the EU, she proposed
a set of principles for the UK–EU discussions. One such principle was that
'we must pay attention to the UK's unique relationship with the Republic
of Ireland and the importance of the peace process in Northern Ireland'
(HMG, 2017b). She elaborated:

> The Republic of Ireland is the only EU member state with a land border with the United Kingdom. We want to avoid a return to a hard border between our two countries ... to make sure that nothing is done to jeopardise the peace process in Northern Ireland, and to continue to uphold the Belfast Agreement. (HMG, 2017b)

In so doing, she was repeating points made to her by the First Minister and deputy First Minister of Northern Ireland a few months beforehand:

> There have been difficult issues relating to the border throughout our history and the peace process. We therefore appreciate your stated determination that the border will not become an impediment to the movement of goods, people and services. It must not become a catalyst for illegal activity ... It is equally important that the border does not create an incentive for those who would wish to undermine the peace process. (TEO, 2016)

For its part, the EU emphatically concurred. The guidelines issued by the European Council for the Withdrawal negotiations also acknowledged 'the unique circumstances on the island of Ireland' and the need to support the 1998 Agreement. As such, it recognised that 'flexible and imaginative solutions will be required, including with the aim of avoiding a hard border, while respecting the integrity of the Union legal order' (European Council, 2017). The common principle was clear; however, the interpretation of this principle was very different between the two sides. What it meant to 'avoid' a 'hard border' on the island of Ireland, let alone what was required to achieve it, was to become one of the most bitterly contested aspects of the UK–EU negotiations.

Even prior to triggering Article 50 to withdraw from the EU, Prime Minister Theresa May had been unequivocal that the UK would leave the single market and the customs union (HMG, 2017a). Not only would there be a customs and a regulatory border between the UK and the EU, but the expectation could only be that divergence between them would increase over time. It was inevitable, therefore, that the challenge of 'avoiding a hard border' between the UK and EU on the island of Ireland would not only be intensely complicated but also increasingly so. From the start of the Brexit negotiations, the UK had been keen to move to discussing the future shape of the UK–EU relationship, whereas the EU was insistent on managing the terms of exit first. For this reason, the withdrawal negotiations were broken into two phases. First, addressing priority issues in withdrawal: EU citizens' rights in the UK (and vice versa), the financial settlement and the Irish border. Then the scope and shape of the future relationship would be outlined. The Joint Report (December 2017) on progress made in phase one of the negotiations set out three scenarios in which the challenge of avoiding a hard Irish border would be addressed. It recognised that the UK's intention was that this could be done through the future UK–EU relationship, even though May's red lines contradicted any prospect of this. So, 'should this not be possible', the second scenario was one in which the UK was to 'propose specific solutions' to address the 'unique circumstances' of the case. Failing agreement on such specific solutions, the default would be that 'the United Kingdom will maintain full alignment with those rules of the Internal Market and the Customs Union' necessary to meet their shared objectives of protecting the 1998 Agreement and supporting north/south cooperation (EC & HMG, 2017: Paragraph 49).

The expectation was that the UK would come up with a draft proposal for scenario one: that is, avoiding a hard border through the future UK–EU relationship. By February 2018, in the absence of any such proposal, the EU took the initiative and published a draft withdrawal agreement which proposed a fall-back solution for Northern Ireland, including it remaining part of the customs territory of the EU (CEC, 2018). The response of Prime Minister May was swift and forthright. No doubt conscious of the 'confidence and supply' agreement she had found it necessary to make with the DUP in order to form a government in June 2017 (HMG, 2017c), May (2018) asserted:

> the draft legal text that the Commission has published, if implemented, would undermine the UK common market and threatens the constitutional integrity of the UK by creating a customs and regulatory border down the Irish sea. No UK Prime Minister could ever agree to it, and I will be making that absolutely clear.

In order to avoid such a situation, the British government's preference was for a temporary customs union with the EU plus a 'common rulebook'. Concerned that such arrangements would predetermine the outcome of the future relationship discussions, the EU was adamant that there needed to be some 'backstop' that was not time-limited and which applied specifically to Northern Ireland. After further difficult deliberations, the UK and the EU announced a Withdrawal Agreement in November 2018 (EC & HMG, 2018). This contained a Protocol on Ireland/Northern Ireland that was described as a 'backstop'. It was a compromise in allowing the UK to be in a single customs territory with the EU, but requiring regulatory alignment between Northern Ireland and the EU. In effect, it was a restricted version of the third scenario in the Joint Report. It was a compromise that pleased neither unionists nor pro-Leave MPs. Unionists objected to Northern Ireland being singled out to align with EU rules, and many MPs baulked at the UK–EU 'single customs territory' proposal.[8] The fact that this backstop could not be unilaterally exited meant that the prospects for 'Global Britain' were seen to rest in the hands of the EU Commission. Unperturbed by the prospects of a 'crash-out' Brexit, the House of Commons voted down the Withdrawal Agreement three times. The deadline for exit was extended beyond 29 March, and the UK returned to the negotiating table with a mandate of finding 'alternative arrangements' to the backstop. May's efforts to avoid a customs border within the UK and to avoid a hard border on the island of Ireland resulted in her losing the confidence of both the DUP and her own party. In July 2019, Boris Johnson succeeded May as party leader and prime minister, pledging to leave the EU without the contentious backstop by the end of October, 'do or die'. Although the rhetoric of the British government became even more hardline and combative, it did nothing to emolliate the need for a UK–EU customs and regulatory border to be drawn somewhere. For these months, as the clock ran down, what would happen to the backstop and also the border in Ireland were the 'great unanswered questions, the issues on which Brexit [would] stand or fall' (Patterson, 2019). What this intense uncertainty meant for residents in the border region was predictably deleterious (Hayward and Komarova, 2019).

A revised Withdrawal Agreement was announced by Prime Minister Boris Johnson and Commission President Jean-Claude Juncker in October 2019, including a new Protocol on Ireland/Northern Ireland (EC & HMG, 2019b). This time, the second scenario envisaged by the Joint Report was put into legally binding form. There were to be 'specific solutions' for Northern Ireland that would enable the absence of new border controls on the island of Ireland. The flipside to this, of course, was that any border controls that were necessary between the UK and the EU would now come to apply between Northern Ireland and Great Britain, that is within the United Kingdom and 'down the Irish Sea'. What this would mean in practice would be largely dependent on the degree to which the UK decided to diverge from the EU after the end of the transition period. The Trade and Cooperation Agreement (TCA) reached on 24 December 2020 contains level-playing-field commitments (e.g. on state aid), but it does not prevent the governments of the UK (including Scotland and Wales as well as Westminster) from setting their own standards in areas of high regulation, such as agri-food (EC & HMG, 2020).[9] The greater the divergence from EU rules in Britain, the greater the need to ensure non-compliant products do not enter the EU single market via Northern Ireland. In effect, to meet its ambition to minimise Britain's ties with the EU, the British government agreed to a hardening of borders all around Northern Ireland.

The Protocol on Ireland/Northern Ireland is a compromise for both the UK and EU

The 'specific solution' for Northern Ireland in the Protocol is unique and even exceptional, not just in the UK but for the EU itself. This is most clearly the case when we consider the position it places Northern Ireland in when it comes to trade. Articles 5–10 of the Protocol are the critical ones here. They cover customs, movement of goods, VAT, the UK internal market, technical regulations (which are listed in Annex 2, in the form of some 290 EU legislative instruments), and the single electricity market on the island of Ireland. Although Northern Ireland remains officially part of the customs territory of the UK and incorporated into future UK trade agreements, the EU's Union Customs Code applies in Northern Ireland. In practice, what this means is a border down the Irish Sea – and one that is to be managed and controlled by the UK authorities, albeit with an EU monitoring 'presence'. All commercial goods moving from Great Britain into Northern Ireland require customs declarations, and some of these goods (those deemed to be at risk of entering the single market) have to have tariffs paid in advance. Products of animal and plant origin moving from Great Britain into Northern Ireland have to be subject to the EU's rules for entry, including Export Health Certificates, plus physical checks on entry through designated and EU-approved Border Control Posts. Northern Ireland will enforce the EU's VAT rules on goods, which do not apply in Britain; this means that sales of goods across the Irish Sea are considered as exports for VAT purposes even though they are occurring within a single state. The

EU's rules on state aid will apply to all trade relevant to the Protocol, most directly on businesses trading in Northern Ireland.

But because Northern Ireland is outside the EU, there will also be a hardening of the Irish land border. Article 11 of the Protocol states that it 'shall be implemented and applied so as to maintain the necessary conditions for continued North-South cooperation', including in such areas as environment, telecommunications, health and education. The Protocol also acknowledges that the UK–Ireland Common Travel Area (which, simply put, gives reciprocal rights to British and Irish citizens in the respective jurisdictions) stands unaffected. However, this is a limited range of 'continuity' amid what otherwise constitutes a huge adjustment. Despite the clear request of the First Minister and deputy First Minster in August 2016, there is now no free movement of services or people across the Irish border. When both the UK and Ireland were EU members, people from all member-states had the right to live, work, study and provide services in either jurisdiction. This had a 'softening' effect on the Irish border. The UK–Ireland Common Travel Area (CTA) stands undiminished but it is far less developed than the EU's single market. The reciprocal rights that British and Irish citizens in Ireland and the UK enjoy through the CTA are insufficient to compensate for the loss of those freedom of movement rights (de Mars et al., 2018). For example, the 2019 memorandum of understanding between the two governments cannot automatically guarantee the recognition of professional qualifications in the CTA, now that it is not provided for in the UK–EU Trade and Cooperation Agreement (Government of Ireland & HMG, 2019). Furthermore, the CTA has no bearing on citizens who are neither British nor Irish. Northern Ireland's economy is particularly vulnerable to the negative impact of reduced migration compared with the rest of the UK (CBI NI, 2018). This is where the Irish border can have a negative effect on Northern Ireland's economy. There was evidence in the lead-up to the UK's withdrawal from the EU that Northern Ireland suffered loss as a result of the 'retreat' across the border by companies and individuals seeking the certainty of EU membership – not least of which is access to labour (Hayward, 2017). Looking ahead, people on the island of Ireland are used to managing the existence of the border in daily life, for example in the use of two currencies. The inconveniences and costs of, for example, mobile phone roaming charges, frontier worker permits, and 'green cards' for motor insurance will be resented but accommodated. However, the consequences of Brexit will not end there.

Just as the process of opening the border through European integration was varied, complex and incremental, so the effects of Northern Ireland being outside the EU will harden the Irish border in varied, complex and incremental ways.

The Protocol will not create a united Ireland by stealth

Because Articles 5 and 7 of the Protocol mean that Northern Ireland effectively remains in the EU's customs union and single market for goods while Britain is outside it, the Irish land border is less 'hard' than that of the Irish Sea border for the movement of goods. This has produced speculation that the all-island economy will grow, as Northern Ireland businesses seize the chance to have 'the best of both worlds'. There is often a subtext to this, which is that such growth will occur by and large at the expense of Northern Ireland's place in the UK's internal market. Unionists and nationalists alike have postulated that growing integration of the all-island economy will ultimately bring closer political unity. Could it be that the long-term outcome of the Protocol – be it by accident or design – is a united Ireland by stealth? Northern Ireland businesses may well adjust supply chains in a way that makes them more oriented to the EU than to Britain – particularly in those highly regulated sectors which will experience most friction in crossing the sea border into Northern Ireland. And going on patterns to date, we can be quite sure that much of that reorientation will begin with the Republic of Ireland (the gravity model of trade is borne out by evidence) (McClelland and Duffy, 2019). But free market access from Northern Ireland into Great Britain (as enabled by the UK Internal Market Act, 2020) will potentially mean that Northern Ireland's position for west to east trade could prove quite attractive for some. The flow of goods from NI to GB could well increase. Moreover, it is important that we do not overlook the fact that borders can be open for some things and hard for others at the same time. There are reasons why the European single market grew to include services, people, capital and digital data, as well as goods. It is far from the case that the whole Northern Ireland economy depends on the movement of goods. Just as opportunities will open up for purchasing from south of the border, so new obstacles will arise for other types of economic growth, particularly in the realm of services. What is more, just as those who claimed (some in horror, some in hope) that the growth of the EU single market would create a closer European polity have not proven to be correct, so we cannot assume that economic integration in some sectors will provoke widespread political and cultural assimilation.

It is important to take lessons from what has happened over the course of the history of the border to date. First, the common UK and EU membership of the single market formed the necessary conditions for the embryonic all-island economy. As early as 1992, at a conference of the Confederation of British Industry in Northern Ireland (of which he was then chair), Sir George Quigley proposed that the European Union should treat the island of Ireland 'as a single entity', 'given the imminence of the single market and worldwide economic trends' (D'Arcy and Dickson, 1995; Phoenix, 2018). The 'negative reaction' that this idea drew from unionist politicians meant that both governments were careful not to openly champion this idea at the time (Phoenix, 2018). Nonetheless, the context of European integration and, later, the conditions of the 1998 Agreement meant that business leaders became increasingly inclined to view an all-island dimension to policy formation in terms of tangible and mutual benefit (Hayward and Magennis, 2014; NWCBRG, 1994). The context of the EU not only enabled such links, but was also the 'safe space' in which to talk about them without political risk. Outwith that environment, there are obstacles to sustaining and growing such links.

And – contrary to the fears of unionists – there is little evidence that cross-border economic integration has a 'spillover' effect into political preference or cultural identity, or even embedded institutional habits of cooperation (Tannam, 1999). Post-1998 Agreement, with both the UK and Ireland part of the EU, and even at the height of economic boom in the south, there was little prospect of an all-island economy overcoming the economic impact of partition (Bradley and Best, 2012). What business networks and cross-border trade can do is 'normalise' cooperation. In contrast to times past, the majority of people on the island of Ireland are no longer afraid or wary of such cooperation. However, post-Brexit, the conditions are far from conducive to integration. Northern Ireland is only partially in the single market, and the effects of being outside the EU will compound over time. Just as was always the case, cross-border cooperation – east/west and north/south – depends on forums as well as habits of communication and cooperation among officials and politicians. Moreover, intergovernmental commitment to enabling such cooperation remains vital (Tannam, 2006). The difficulty for Northern Ireland post-Brexit and post-Protocol is that the degree of integration across both its sea and land borders now depends, in no small part, on the relationship between the UK and the EU.

Notes

1. This image of a Fianna Fáil advert in the 1972 referendum on accession to the EEC is reproduced here with kind permission of Fianna Fáil.
2. Notably, it was also charged with considering the EU dimension of such policies and of ensuring that its common NSMC views 'are taken into account and represented appropriately at relevant EU meetings'. This role will continue in a different way, with the Protocol allowing the UK–EU Specialised Committee to 'examine proposals concerning the implementation and application of this Protocol' from the NSMC and north/south implementation bodies (Article 14).
3. The Agreement contained an Annex for this section which suggested a wide range of areas for north/south cooperation and implementation. It was also envisaged that there would be a Joint Parliamentary Forum and an Independent Consultative Forum to accompany the work of the NSMC; as with the Civic Forum in Strand One, these measures have not been implemented.
4. The amendment to Article 29 of the Irish Constitution states: 'Any institution established by or under the Agreement may exercise the powers and functions conferred on it in respect of all or any part of the island of Ireland.'
5. Sinn Féin have long made a referendum on Irish unification a mantra of their election campaigns and press statements. Calling the bluff of republicans was the rationale given by both UUP First Minister David Trimble in March 2002 and DUP MLA Arlene Foster in 2013, when saying that they would be willing to see Sinn Féin's demands for a border poll realised. Foster (2013) said that she thought the results of such a poll would 'consolidate the union'. However, just four years later, as leader of the DUP, Foster posited that maintaining the union with the UK was 'by far' the most important issue in the upcoming general election and urged that a majority of unionists MPs should be returned from Northern Ireland in order to take a 'border poll off the agenda for generations'. Her message found fertile soil in the 'Brexit' election, which saw the (temporary) eradication of 'middle ground' MPs from Northern Ireland, with the DUP taking ten seats and Sinn Féin the remaining seven.
6. Although there has not been a dramatic growth in support for unification in the Republic of Ireland (which has remained more or less around 70 per cent since the 1970s), what has changed is the hope and expectation that this is not a remote prospect. An exit poll conducted during the 2020 Irish general election

found 57 per cent support for holding unification referendums within the next five years (WGURII, 2020: 3.43).

7. That is, 59 per cent nationalist, 1 per cent unionist, 37 per cent neither in 2015 compared with 59 per cent nationalist, 0 per cent unionist, 39 per cent four years later in 2019 (Northern Ireland Life and Times Surveys).

8. For more on the response of political parties in Northern Ireland to EU membership and Brexit see Murphy (2018).

9. Indeed, the TCA does not even go as far as the EU's trade agreements with Canada or Japan in this area, given that it does not allow for sanitary and phytosanitary measures (i.e. controls used to protect humans, animals and plants from disease, pests and contaminants) in the UK to be recognised as equivalent to those of the EU. This would allow testing and certification performed by the UK on food products to be accepted as meeting the standards required for entry to the EU. Sanitary and phytosanitary (SPS) controls at a border entail documentary, identity and physical checks on animal- and plant-related produce and are costly, rigorous and time consuming.

what should we do?

Appreciate what it means to 'control' a border

Have borders ever been more popular political touchstones than in this age, one in which our social worlds are so virtual, digital and globalised? Perhaps this is no coincidence. The idea of 'taking back control', of putting limits to what shapes our lives, has a certain logic in the face of seemingly relentless change. It is expedient for governments to paint sources of insecurity as coming from outside, rather than from within. The danger of these threats feels all the greater because they are often invisible, erratic and unexpected: terrorism, ecological disaster, a mutating virus. The 2025 UK Border Strategy assumes that an evermore complete reliance on scientific technologies and administrative expertise in border management will lead it to develop 'the world's most effective border' (HMG, 2020b).[1] However, stricter and more heavily enforced border controls cannot resolve the problems of insecurity. In fact, somewhat inconveniently for the 'build a wall' brigade, effective border security depends on cooperation and information sharing with relevant authorities and agencies in other countries, as well as internally. No matter which way you look at it, even in terms of security, borders are lines of connection.

Put in its simplest terms, controlling a border is about managing flows across it. These flows can take various forms: people, goods, capital, data, services, and even biosecurity hazards. There are three elements to border control in this process (as seen in Figure 4.1). Underpinning it all is the knowledge of what is crossing the border.[2] This is why so much of border control is about data sharing and analytics. The second element is to be sure that what is crossing is allowed to do so – that it meets the rules for entry. And, if it does not, the final element is the ability to prevent its moving across the border. These elements relate to one another, and can become more or less important depending on context. The nature of the challenge depends on the nature of the border, the type of flows being controlled and the conditions in which the border regime is being operationalised.

Effective border management requires buy-in not only from traders but also from a social environment which broadly accepts the need for the border controls. This is always going to be a tricky prospect in the context of Ireland/Northern Ireland, whether we are talking about the Irish Sea or land border. The unique circumstances on the island of Ireland mean that any change to the requirements for crossing either border, or experience of doing so, will be viewed with suspicion. It is near inevitable that one or more of the political parties sharing power in Northern Ireland will seize upon any border-related matter – and stridently at that. Any border management regime needs to meet the test of acceptability as well as feasibility. This should take into account the principle that people of all views in Northern Ireland wish to see as little change as possible to movement across its borders with Great Britain or with Ireland

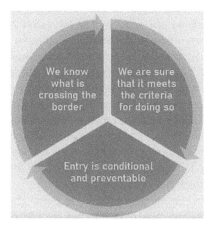

Figure 4.1 Managing flows across a border

(Garry et al., 2018). This is the fundamental difficulty for Northern Ireland post-Brexit: nobody wanted to see either border become harder, but there are new frictions across both the Irish Sea and the land border. This was an effort to avoid a zero-sum outcome but it is inevitably seen in win/lose terms by both unionists and nationalists – each of whom consider themselves to have lost.

Throw technological solutions into the Irish Sea

In November 2017, the European Parliament Committee on Constitutional Affairs hosted a workshop in an amphitheatre in the Paul-Henri Spaak Building on the subject of 'The implications of Brexit on the Irish border'. Three reports had been commissioned by the Committee on the topic, and the authors presented them to a large audience of MEPs that afternoon.[3] One was titled 'Smart Border 2.0' and the author, customs expert Lars Karlsson, made a pitch for:

> the implementation of a new border solution that serves both sides of the border with maximum predictability, speed and security and with a minimum burden and cost for traders and travellers … supported by state-of-the-art technology. (Karlsson, 2017: 10)

Several MEPs present welcomed a scenario in which the Irish border would be managed through technical surveillance and mobile inspection units. They were not alone. Since that point, the 'smart border' technological fix to the 'Irish border problem' has been trumpeted far and wide. Most notably, it constituted a major part of the report of the think tank Prosperity UK (2019) which offered 'alternative arrangements' to the 'backstop' in the first version of the Withdrawal Agreement.[4] It sought the means by which to allow divergence for the whole of the UK from the EU's customs code and regulatory standards at the same time as keeping the Irish border as invisible and frictionless as possible. In the end, given the nature of the conundrum, the proposed alternatives proved implausible. The Protocol on Northern Ireland/Ireland was the resulting compromise. Critics of the Protocol, including the most fervent advocates for a 'hard Brexit', continue to claim that the alternative to it remains a 'smart' Irish border.

The prospect of a fully electronic environment for customs facilitation, aided by the use of technology and remote inspections, is not a complete fantasy. However, it is important to recognise what this would require. As a first step, there would need to be detailed data on flows across the border, plus the algorithms to process it and the means of sharing it between respective border agencies. Advance cargo information would be essential for risk analysis, and this is much more difficult to enforce for an open land border than for sea or air borders (which have specified entry points and which take time to traverse).[5] There are 208 roads across the Irish border, and the 10 major ones are crossed approximately 95,000 times every day (DTTaS & DfI, 2018; UUEPC, 2017: 32). Moreover, the more regulatory divergence between the states either side of the border, the more rigorous the process of verification needs to be. Detailed data does not substitute for capacity to perform physical inspections at some point, and such inspections can require specialised facilities (e.g. for veterinary or biological checks). If goods are deemed not to meet the criteria for entry, then it should be possible to prevent them doing so. The more crossing points there are and the more opportunities for contraband to be moved or diverted, the more difficult the task for border agencies.

Technology can serve three core functions when it comes to customs facilitation. First, it can speed up the submission and processing of information. In particular, this is intended to minimise errors, to reduce personnel time and costs, and to reduce friction and queues on the border crossing. This can take the form of smartphone apps, which include information for the customs agencies (e.g. details on the driver, the consignment) and information to the driver (e.g. that permission is granted for entry). Barcode scanning can also ensure that a great deal of information can be shared quickly and with minimum fuss, and the potential to link to other identified piece of information (e.g. Automatic Number Plate Recognition (ANPR) of the truck). This is just about the transfer of information. All these technologies are in use to facilitate the movement of goods across the Irish Sea in the operationalisation of the Protocol.

Secondly, technology can be used to confirm when a vehicle (or a container or item on that vehicle) crosses a particular point at a particular time. This can be done by measures that require either some connection between information at the entry point (e.g. ANPR, Radio Frequency Identification, Bluetooth, beacon tags – all of which require some physical infrastructure at the crossing point) or continual tracking (e.g. via GPS).

The greater the distance enabled between the vehicle of interest and the receiver, the greater the cost of the technology. As with the example above, such technology does not confirm what is precisely in the vehicle/container. It relies on the data submitted in advance about the consignment being accurate and detailed. This technology has limited use for managing a regulatory border, and this is why there are border control posts and physical inspections required of some goods entering Northern Ireland from Great Britain.

Finally, non-intrusive inspection technologies can be used to check for smuggling.[6] Modern drive-through container X-ray scanners are capable of scanning upwards of 100 vehicles per hour – and their capacity is improving all the time, mainly due to advances in military technology, which is where the origins of much border management technology lies. Artificial intelligence can be used to assess a scanned image of contents of a container in order to determine whether it matches what would be expected in the declared consignment. If a potential problem is identified, however, the vehicle then needs to be directed to secondary inspection where it can undergo a more detailed type of scanning and/or physical inspection of the container. Inspection requires not only personnel but also equipment and facilities for unloading and storage, for example with refrigerated capacity. No non-intrusive technology can determine whether a box of beefburgers actually contains horsemeat, or whether crates of apples have been treated with a dangerous pesticide, or whether a 'best before' label has been tampered with.

Ultimately, the challenge for 'smart solutions' lies with the nature of the problems they are meant to solve. These problems increase with, for example, divergence in rules applying either side of the border, the number of entry/exit points, the complexity of the trade flows (e.g. highly regulated goods), and the scale of adjustment required. Exacerbating the challenge is the social environment. There is acute political and cultural sensitivity to any change in border management, land or sea, in Northern Ireland. If political leaders reject the rationale for a new border regime (be it because they oppose Brexit or the Protocol designed to manage it), then this makes its implementation all the more difficult. This is the unhappy conundrum of Northern Ireland. Politicians who advocate 'technological solutions' do so for the border that they are ideologically most inclined to see as a boundary than a bridge. Thus the debate is rarely about the capacity of the solutions to meet the problems, and all too often about the relative significance of the 'two' communities' identity and concerns. In purely technical terms, it is clear that 'smart solutions' hold more feasibility for the movement of goods across the Irish Sea than the Irish land border, but they cannot make any border 'frictionless'.

Equip the UK–EU relationship for their joint responsibility to Northern Ireland

Apart from its implications for border management and the economy, the Protocol has transformed the conditions for the governance of Northern Ireland. From now on, the region will be directly affected by decisions that are made by the UK and the EU. The UK–EU Joint Committee, initially co-chaired by Michael Gove (and then David Frost) for the UK government and Maroš Šefčovič for the EU Commission, has responsibility for decisions that will affect all three strands of the 1998 Agreement. As such, what it decides will have implications for what happens across Northern Ireland's borders. Indeed, according to Article 11(2), the Joint Committee is charged with keeping 'under constant review the extent to which the implementation and application of this Protocol maintains the necessary conditions for North-South cooperation'. There is no definition of what 'the necessary conditions' are. But this could affect policy and practice in both the Republic of Ireland and Northern Ireland. The future conditions for cooperation across the Irish border will no longer be only a north/south or British–Irish concern; they will be shaped by the UK–EU relationship. What is more, the Joint Committee will also affect east/west relations too. Under Article 6 ('The protection of the UK internal market'), the Joint Committee is given responsibility for ensuring the facilitation of trade within the UK:

> the Union and the United Kingdom shall use their best endeavours to facilitate the trade between Northern Ireland and other parts of the United Kingdom ... The Joint Committee shall keep the application of this paragraph under constant review and shall adopt appropriate recommendations with a view to avoiding controls at the ports and airports of Northern Ireland to the extent possible. (Art. 6.ii)

A particular challenge in this regard, of course, is that the facilitation of trade within the UK will become increasingly difficult as the regulatory regimes

of Great Britain and the EU diverge. Because Northern Ireland's regulatory regime will remain aligned to the EU's in matters relating to trade, and
because the UK–EU Trade and Cooperation Agreement allows regulatory
divergence between Great Britain and the EU, there will be increasing bar-
riers to trade within the UK internal market. The UK has legislated for this.
The Taxation Bill (2020) and the UK Internal Market Act (2020) both allow
for customs and regulatory controls on the movement of goods between
Britain and Northern Ireland. Such controls will in theory become more
significant as any part of Great Britain decides to diverge from the EU
standards (e.g. in the use of pesticides, or genetic engineering in plants)
or as the EU increases its standards (e.g. banning single-use plastics).
Although Article 6.ii may stress the intention of 'avoiding controls', the
more important four words are: '*to the extent possible*'. What the Protocol
means for east/west movement across the Irish Sea depends on what the
UK and the EU can agree and the manner in which these decisions are
enforced.

The British–Irish relationship remains of fundamental importance, but
it has been superseded by the UK–EU relationship. Northern Ireland is
peripheral to both the UK and the EU in almost every way but it is com-
pletely dependent on their capacity to communicate, trust and agree
with each other. As with the British–Irish relationship, the fragile balance
within the region is now vulnerable to tensions, animosities and (as we
have already seen) misjudgements between the two sides. There are fears
that both the UK and the EU could use Northern Ireland to 'make a point'
to or, indeed, about the other. The peace process depended on the British and Irish governments, and political leaders, consciously refusing to
employ such rhetoric and tactics (Arthur, 2000). The UK and EU need to
acknowledge and address their duty of care towards Northern Ireland as
co-guarantors of the Protocol. This begins with a clear-eyed recognition of
the compromises required, but also of the ongoing need for 'flexible and
imaginative solutions'. As with the 1998 Agreement, these will be needed
in modes of governance as well as in operational adjustments.

Both the UK and EU have approached problems with the Protocol as
if they are primarily technical matters, but there is a much more fundamental difficulty with it: a lack of legitimacy. As an international agreement
that encapsulated a complicated compromise, this was always going to
be a challenge. The legitimacy of the 1998 Agreement is based on both
'input' and 'output': that is, who is involved in decision-making and what

the outcomes of those decisions are. But there is no direct decision-making role for Northern Ireland anticipated or provided for in the Protocol. Northern Ireland representatives can only be present in meetings of the Joint Committee and Specialised Committee if they are invited by the UK government and if members of the Irish government are also there. The UK government has claimed that the 'consent vote' constitutes 'the democratic principle at the heart of the Protocol' (HMG, 2020a: para 4). This is a vote to be taken by the Assembly every four or (if the vote receives cross-community support) eight years on the continued application of Articles 5–10 of the Protocol, namely those which give rise to customs and regulatory checks across the Irish Sea. If MLAs vote to disapply these articles, the matter of how to meet the objectives of the Protocol (i.e. to avoid a hard Irish border and protect the 1998 Agreement) will return to the level of UK and EU deliberation (Phinnemore, 2020). This is, however, far from sufficient as a means of giving the Protocol legitimacy. There is a need, at the very least, for 'throughput' legitimacy, that is some means by which Northern Ireland can shape how decisions are made regarding the Protocol (Hayward et al., 2020). At the very least, it would be necessary to apply the principle of subsidiarity, with the aim being to take decisions at a level as close to those affected as possible. This poses an opportunity for a new, if modest, type of 'constitutional innovation' in both the UK and EU.

Learn from the cross-border (mis)handling of the coronavirus pandemic

The coronavirus pandemic exemplified the porosity of national borders. The first case of COVID-19 in Northern Ireland was diagnosed on 27 February 2020. It came in a person who arrived at Dublin Airport from Italy and then travelled north on a train across the Irish border. The second case was in someone who had been in contact with a victim of the virus in Great Britain. In the fortnight that followed, the number of cases in Northern Ireland, in the Republic of Ireland and in Great Britain grew exponentially. The World Health Organization urged governments to act. On 11 March, Taoiseach Leo Varadkar announced strict measures in the Republic of Ireland to tackle the spread of coronavirus, but, much to the irritation of the First Minister, his government had failed to notify the Northern Ireland Executive in advance. Meanwhile, the guidance of the chief medical officer in the north matched that of his counterpart in the UK government: do nothing drastic for now. Northern Ireland's ministers were caught by the fact that the UK and Irish scientific advice was conflicting. Their political responses were shaped by ideological preferences. The nationalist parties in Northern Ireland, Sinn Féin and the SDLP, called for a common approach on the island of Ireland. But the other three parties in the power-sharing Executive – the Alliance Party, Democratic Unionist Party and Ulster Unionist Party – did not want to move against the medical advice that tallied with the view in London. The Northern Ireland Executive was paralysed by indecision. This was particularly frustrating for all-island organisations, such as sporting bodies, and for those living in border communities; many decided to err on the side of caution and adhere to the stricter rules of the Republic. An emergency session of the North/South Ministerial Council on 14 March 2020 helped to ease political tensions, but proved unable to alter the fundamental problem, which was the gulf between the UK and Irish governments on the matter. It was not until the end of March 2020 that the UK government's Secretary of State for Northern Ireland, Brandon Lewis, the Tánaiste, the First and deputy First Ministers of Northern Ireland, and the two ministers for health held their first conference call on COVID-19. In the joint statement after, the ministers promised:

> cooperation for the practical and mutual benefit of the people living in both jurisdictions on the island of Ireland will be taken forward. [And] agreed that all cooperation will be based on the need to be agile, open and consistent and that close and ongoing contact will be maintained North-South and East-West.

The experience and management of the coronavirus pandemic has revealed both the necessity and the complexity of British–Irish and north/south cooperation. First, it has confirmed the intimate connections that exist between Northern Ireland and the Republic of Ireland, Northern Ireland and Great Britain, and, through the Common Travel Area, the Republic and the UK. In practice, this means that policies and practices regarding COVID-19 in Ireland and Great Britain have a direct impact on those formulated for Northern Ireland. The flipside of integration is, of course, the difficulty of imposing restrictions on movement. The pandemic led to an unprecedented 'hardening' of borders within the UK. The Welsh government's restrictions on entry to Wales from England were enforced with police checks at the border. Travel between Scotland and the rest of the UK was prohibited by law. Yet Northern Ireland refused to put in place any controls or checks on movement across either of its borders. If ever vain symbolism triumphed over real need, it was then. Even in a global pandemic, the Executive approached border-related decisions as matters of ideological integrity, not public responsibility. And when, in February 2021, the Garda Síochána introduced fines for those crossing the Irish border (after already haven taken similar measures for restricting movement between counties in Ireland), it was quickly seized upon by unionist politicians as a sign that the Irish border could be 'hard' after all (Robinson, 2021b).

Secondly, as well as differences in scientific advice and political preference, a coherent policy response on the island of Ireland was delayed by failures to communicate in a timely manner with counterparts on the other side of the border. It was not until February 2021 – a year on from the first cases of COVID-19 on the island which came from travel across these borders – that an 'interim solution' was found to manage the issue of people arriving in one jurisdiction on the island whose final destination was in the other jurisdiction. The difficulty of coming to this agreement centred on the sharing of passenger information between authorities in the different jurisdictions (McClements and Bray, 2021). The fact that such a practical matter took so long to address even in the face of the gravest danger to public health for generations suggests that the capacity for north/south cooperation remains underdeveloped in key areas. Now that Northern Ireland is outside the EU, we have to assume that the means of such cooperation will only become more difficult.

Protect the democratic integrity of potential unification referendums

The principle of consent means that Northern Ireland will remain 'in its entirety' 'part of the United Kingdom' until such a time as a majority vote in a poll on whether 'Northern Ireland should cease to be part of the United Kingdom and form part of a united Ireland'.[7] To support the 1998 Agreement is to accept that the aspirations of nationalism are not presently realised and will not be without the consent of a majority in Northern Ireland; it is equally to accept the potential thwarting of unionist aspirations in the future, with no prospect of their being realised after that. The aspirations of unionism require continuity; the aspirations of nationalism require change, and the Agreement provides a means for this. It obliges the Secretary of State for Northern Ireland to direct the holding of such a poll 'if at any time it appears likely to him [*sic*] that a majority of those voting would express a wish' that Northern Ireland 'form part of a united Ireland'. The 1998 Agreement has it that, if there is no such a majority vote in a referendum, another cannot be held within a period of seven years. But if there is a majority vote, then:

> the Secretary of State shall lay before Parliament such proposals to give effect to that wish as may be agreed between Her Majesty's Government in the United Kingdom and the Government of Ireland. (Northern Ireland Act, 1998: Art. 1ii)

This is about as much as is absolutely clear from the text of the 1998 Agreement and the Act that puts it into UK law. It leaves a very great deal that is still to be determined.

Possibly shaken by the lessons as well as the consequences of the Brexit referendum, there has since been a growth of interest in what a future united Ireland might look like. This has come in the form of civic groupings either campaigning for a referendum (such as Ireland's Future, Trade Unionists for a New and United Ireland, or Yes for Unity), or seeking simply to raise the profile of the issue (such as the Constitutional Conversations group, Shared Ireland, or Think32). There is also academic engagement in the topic, with the ARINS project (Analysis and Research on Ireland North and South) coordinated by the Royal Irish Academy and the University of Notre Dame, with academics on an advisory board from every higher education institution on the island. And the Irish government itself founded the Shared Island Unit in the Department of the Taoiseach in 2020, supported by a budget of half a million euros, to invest in research, dialogue and infrastructure to help 'build consensus around a shared future'. The remit of the Shared Island Unit is carefully framed as being distinct from any 'preparation' for Irish unification. However, if and when such preparation were to take place, the enormity of the task should not be underestimated. Detailed plans on how to integrate and manage the economy, social security and welfare, national debt, health, education, pensions, policing, security, public utilities and services on the island will be needed. These are in addition to fundamental matters such as the status and integration of political representation, civil service, and law and the courts. There is debate as to whether the institutions of Northern Ireland will or should continue in a united Ireland (cf. Humphreys, 2018: 106-116; WGURII, 2020: 9.42).

Before any of that is considered, there are a number of issues around the essential mechanics of holding any referendum on unification that need to be determined. In 2019–2021, a Working Group on unification referendums on the island of Ireland was convened by the Constitution Unit of University College London to look in detail at what might be deduced from the 1998 Agreement, and the legal, socio-political and historical context of the UK and Ireland (WGURII, 2020).[8] The work revealed the extent to which the Agreement and British and Irish law is silent or ambiguous on the process of what is often casually referred to as 'calling a border poll'. For example, the grounds upon which the Secretary of State will base any judgement as to whether there is 'likely' to be a majority of people who would vote in favour of Irish unification needs to be determined. Each source of potential evidence raises further questions that would need to be considered in advance: survey and poll data (e.g. what sampling method, how many such polls should show a pro-unity majority); voting in elections (e.g. seats returned, first-preference votes cast); or votes in the Northern Ireland Assembly for the Secretary of State to hold a referendum (e.g. what if members abstained?). Any assessment of evidence of this sort should bear in mind that the intention should be for a majority vote in any referendum to reflect the majority view of the population. There is a risk of abstention from a future referendum (as in 1973), and a unionist boycott of a poll would guarantee a majority in a referendum. That may trigger the process of a transfer of sovereignty, but it would not be a sure foundation for the unity of a 'united' Ireland. As such, the grounds and conditions for the calling of any referendum should validate the judgement that the majority view in Northern Ireland as a whole is for Irish unification.

Secondly, the input of the Irish government into decisions prior to and after a referendum on Irish unification needs to be properly considered. The Agreement recognises the right of 'the people of the island of Ireland alone' to exercise 'their right of self-determination on the basis of consent, freely and concurrently given, North and South'. The revised Article 3 of Bunreacht na hÉireann confirms that 'a united Ireland shall be brought about only by peaceful means with the consent of a majority of the people, democratically expressed, in both jurisdictions in the island'. This leads us to expect that a referendum on Irish unification in the Republic of Ireland would be concurrent with any in Northern Ireland. This raises more matters that would ideally be agreed between the British and Irish governments in advance, including the timing, franchise, format and questions in such referendums. The Working Group argues that there is no existing legal provision for a franchise in Northern Ireland for a referendum. If the existing franchise for Assembly elections is not adopted (e.g. in order to lower the age of franchise, or to include EU or Commonwealth citizens) then the Secretary of State would need to specify it more than a year in advance of the referendum (according to the Venice Commission Code of Good Practice on Referendums) (WGURII, 2020: 15.38). The same principle is true of the franchise for a referendum in the Republic of Ireland. If it is changed (e.g. to include non-resident Irish citizens), then the closer this happens to a referendum on unification, the greater the risk of being seen to manipulate the outcome. Similarly, although the questions will necessarily be different between the two referendums, it would be best if there could be deliberation in advance of their being set in order to avoid confusion (e.g. in which a Yes vote in the Republic would be for Irish unification, and a Yes vote in Northern Ireland would be to remain in the UK). Even more significantly, the British and Irish governments should liaise about what processes should happen before and after a referendum, including when and how the details of a united Ireland would be agreed, and at what point sovereignty would be transferred, if there were a majority vote for unification.

Finally, there is an urgent need to address the current weaknesses in legislation around the referendum campaigns. For a referendum of such consequence, it would be vital to ensure that the campaign rules and procedures are robust and secure for democratic credibility. As things stand at the moment, as Peter Geoghegan (2020: 7) succinctly put it, 'the corruption of democracy is as much about perfectly legal abuse as it is law-breaking malfeasance'. The problems centre upon one thing: distortion. There are new methods abroad for corrupting the pillars of democracy: truth, representativeness, transparency and accountability. Current legislation in the UK and Ireland is woefully inadequate to regulate the online means through which campaigns (and untruths) gather momentum:

Algorithms can aggregate the innocent behaviour of millions of online users into highly skewed discourses. Campaigners can exploit new opportunities for targeted messaging and circumvent the quality filters provided by traditional journalism. Malign actors can sow disruption to suit their own purposes. (WGURII, 2020: 17.4)

Online advertising is largely unregulated and money spent online by campaign groups can be easily invisible, leaving elections vulnerable to foreign interference (Electoral Commission, 2018). There is also a risk of external interference and distortion in referendum campaigns through both the use of artificial intelligence and abuse of residency rules for donors. Related to this, there is a pressing need to improve the practices of referendum campaign management, including tightening reporting requirements and increasing penalties for those found guilty of breaking those rules (ICR, 2018). If we presume that there will be concurrent referendums, north and south, this adds a new dimension to the challenge. The UK and Ireland have different rules and approaches regarding referendum campaigns. For example, with regard to funding, the UK has controls on spending *by* groups, while Irish rules concentrate on donations *to* groups. Neither system is immune from distortion or corruption. Geoghegan (2020: 306) summarises the present threats to democracy as 'disinformation, dark money and spiralling polarisation'. Referendums on Irish unification would be liable to the worst effects of such malaise unless the British and Irish governments act quickly to secure and protect the integrity of their electoral systems.

Recognise the diversity that a united Ireland would have to unite

whatever choice is freely exercised by a majority of the people of Northern Ireland, the power of the sovereign government with jurisdiction there shall be exercised with rigorous impartiality on behalf of all the people in the diversity of their identities and traditions and shall be founded on the principles of full respect for, and equality of, civil, political, social and cultural rights, of freedom from discrimination for all citizens, and of parity of esteem and of just and equal treatment for the identity, ethos, and aspirations of both communities. (Agreement between the British and Irish Governments, 1998: Art. 1iii)

In the two decades since the 1998 Agreement, it has often been pertinent to ask whether the British government is exercising its power in Northern Ireland 'with rigorous impartiality'. If there were to be a united Ireland, this same duty will be required of the Irish government, but it will be a much more complicated task. For a start, it will not be merely about parity of esteem between unionism and nationalism – not least because unionism as a political *aspiration* will no longer hold much purchase. Instead, it will require genuine recognition of 'the diversity' of 'identities and traditions' on the island of Ireland; this would bring opportunities as well as challenges for the Irish state. It is also important to note that, even in the event of Irish unification, the British government remains a co-guarantor of the 1998 Agreement and the British state will continue to have a synergetic relationship with Ireland as a consequence.

The Agreement confirms the birthright of 'all the people of Northern Ireland' to 'identify themselves and be accepted as Irish or British, or both'. Were there to be a change to the constitutional status of Northern Ireland, then the birthright to be identified (and accepted) as British in a united Ireland would have to remain. This poses a fascinating challenge for both the British and Irish states. In the first instance, it potentially means that 'Northern Ireland' will continue to exist as a territorial unit of significance. There is much debate about whether this is necessarily so in terms of the continuation of the 'Strand One' institutions (Humphreys, 2018; WGURII, 2020); this point about citizenship is slightly different. It means that, presumably, being born in the six counties would constitute eligibility for British citizenship if at least one parent was a British or Irish citizen at the time of birth.[9] This has more consequences for Irish law than British nationality law, because it exposes differences in rights between British and Irish citizens in Ireland. In a united Ireland, there will need to be no discrimination between, and equal treatment of, British and Irish citizens. The equal treatment would mean that British citizens (at the very least, those born in the six counties) would have the right to vote in national referendums and in European Parliament elections (something that British citizens in Ireland cannot currently do). Another matter that would also have to be resolved would be the issue exposed by the Emma DeSouza case, namely the automatic conferral of citizenship onto those born in the six counties. Given Irish government ministers' support for DeSouza's argument against people born in Northern Ireland being automatically conferred with British citizenship (Cochrane, 2020: 59–61), would the government of a united

Ireland also object to people born in the six counties being automatically conferred with Irish citizenship?

Of course, citizenship should not be conflated with national identity. The majority of people in Northern Ireland today think of themselves as being *both* British and Irish, to varying degrees.[10] This an interesting consequence of a steady process of change over time. When Richard Rose (1971) conducted a survey of identities held in Northern Ireland, he found that 39 per cent of Protestants described their identity as British, 20 per cent as Irish and 32 per cent as 'Ulster'. In contrast, although 15 per cent of Catholics described themselves as British, 76 per cent said they were Irish and 5 per cent as 'Ulster'. About 2–3 per cent of both Catholics and Protestants said that their identity was both British and Irish (Rose, 1971). Over the course of the conflict, the shift in Protestant identity away from 'Ulster' and 'Irish' towards 'British' was striking; 20 years on from Rose's study, over two-thirds of Protestants described themselves as British (Moxon-Browne, 1991). Today, younger Protestants increasingly favour the Northern Irish identity in place of a British one (Tonge and Gomez, 2015). McNicholl et al. (2019) found that those who describe themselves as 'Northern Irish' tend to be more supportive of power-sharing, more supportive of social mixing and more moderate on the constitutional question than those with exclusively British or Irish identities. This is borne out by findings from the 2019 Northern Ireland Life and Times Survey. Just over half of the Catholic respondents described themselves as 'Irish only' and 61 per cent of Protestant respondents described themselves as 'British only'. These groups were twice as likely as their co-religionists with a 'Northern Irish' identity to describe themselves as 'nationalist' or 'unionist' respectively. What this goes to show is that Northern Ireland contains a spectrum of identities, and that these can change according to external conditions and by generation. More to the point, if there were to be a united Ireland tomorrow, a significant proportion of its population would hold an exclusively British identity (around 12 per cent, including those already in the Republic of Ireland) and around 1 in 5 of its population would hold some form of British identity. This would be no inconsiderable challenge for the official national identity of the Irish state. In principle, it could be risen to by bearing in mind two things. The first is that, according to the 1998 Agreement, British and Irish identities can be held to be equally legitimate and compatible. If this is the case in Northern Ireland within the Union, it should be equally so in a united Ireland. The second is that the notion of Ireland or 'Irish' as ethnically or nationally 'homogenous' is due for an overhaul anyway.

In a united Ireland, the proportion of the population with a British-only identity would be around the same as the current proportion of its population who do not have Irish nationality. The 2016 census showed that the population of the Republic of Ireland continues to grow and to become increasingly diverse.[11] Of around 4.76 million residents, 11.6 per cent of the population are non-Irish nationals (with 2.2 per cent holding dual nationality), and 17.3 per cent of the population having been born abroad (CSO, 2017). As had been the case since 2011, British citizens constituted the third largest nationality group (2.2 per cent of the population), with Polish forming the second largest (2.7 per cent). Although there are over 200 nationalities resident in Ireland, 69 per cent of non-Irish nationals come from just 10 countries (all EU, which then included the UK). Of the 12.9 per cent who spoke a foreign language at home, almost a third were born in Ireland (CSO, 2017). The population in Northern Ireland (around 1.89 million) has not grown nearly as quickly nor as diversely as that of its neighbour. In 2018, non-Irish EU nationals constituted 3.3 per cent of the population and non-EU nationals around 2.7 per cent (Oxford Economics, 2020). The most significant source of immigration to Northern Ireland in the past 20 years has been the European Union. Indeed, the enlargement of the EU coincided with the change in the trend of net migration for Northern Ireland, with in-flows greater than out-flows from 2004 for a period of six years (NISRA, 2019). The peak of inward migration reached before the economic crash of 2008 has not been matched since, and there is little expectation that it will be matched in the foreseeable future, given the UK's exit from the EU. Nevertheless, it is evident that Northern Ireland contains many more than 'two communities', and its people of many ethnicities, languages and cultures are equally invested in its future. Any process of Irish unification cannot be about assimilation or homogeneity, but one of building unity and equality among 'all the people in the diversity of their identities and traditions'.

Listen to those in the border region

I think because we were so far south the rest of Northern Ireland didn't take us with them ... They kind of just left us behind. They didn't really see us as being a factor or something to really consider. So when the peace process was happening … the south didn't really care about us and neither did the north, and we were kind of a bit of both. (Resident of south Armagh who grew up in the post-Agreement context; interview with the author, November 2020)

For a comparatively small country, the persistent neglect of the Irish border region by the power-holding centres is quite astonishing. This is in some ways typical of centre–periphery dynamics, overlaid to some degree by urban–rural difference too. Partition and the discomfort and unease this caused in the political psyche, both north and south, no doubt contributed to this. Such discomfort tended towards disdain in some quarters, and exaggerated sectarianism in others. Even though familial and cultural and economic ties endured, the broad sense of collective unfamiliarity with 'the other jurisdiction' was fed by official discourses which defined 'us' against 'them' over the border. All this was compounded by the Troubles, which led to the military and material (not to mention emotional) breaking of cross-border connections. All of these processes, over the decades, had their worst effect closest to the border. Part of this was the sense of 'other-ness' that existed north and south towards the border region. It still lingers. And so unionists of the north-east Antrim are being genuine when they say that they think a hard Irish border would make no difference – they very rarely go near it. Just as teenagers in Monaghan say that people in Cork and Dublin do not really 'understand just how close people actually are to the border' and how changes to it would 'be really difficult for everyone, both up north and here' (quoted in Hayward, 2018: 76). Media and political discourse during the coronavirus pandemic brought latent habits of partitionism to the fore. If a policy was deemed to be successful (e.g. lockdown, vaccination rollout), some commentators and politicians contrasted it favourably with that of the other jurisdiction; equally, failures of policy were sometimes blamed upon the other side too.[12] The complex and liminal experience of those in the border region was consistently overlooked.

The neglect of the border region is reflected in the deficiencies in infrastructure and investment there. The New Decade, New Approach document that got the power-sharing Executive and Assembly up and running in January 2020 after a three-year hiatus contained ambitious proposals for the border region. The Irish government once again utilised its National Development plan to invest in connectivity across the island (including in projects such as the A5 road scheme that were 'met' with NI Executive funding) and in border communities, including in greenways, education links and reconciliation projects. Being geographically peripheral to the hubs of economic growth in Dublin and Belfast, the border region has suffered the consequences of back-to-back development (with economic policies on one side of the border paying little heed to the consequences for the other side). Combined with the legacy of conflict, chronic unemployment and poor infrastructure, the border region remains in particular need of private enterprise, sustained international aid and coordinated investment (Bradley and Best, 2012; Buchanan, 2014). Such actions are needed to support, not substitute for, ambition and strategy at the local level across the border region. It is striking how the response to Brexit from the border region has been characterised by strong and positive political leadership among district and county councils. In the east border region, 11 local authorities commissioned a report to examine the prospects for the border corridor between Belfast and Dublin – as urged 30 years previously by George Quigley (UUEPC, 2017). The North West City Region is underpinned by a strategic growth partnership involving officials from central government, north and south, and by a development group that formalises cooperation between senior management and elective representatives from Derry City and Strabane District Council and Donegal County Council. The close cross-border partnership in policy-making and resource allocation across the EU border also involves private sector bodies and third-level institutions in the region (NWRDG, 2017). And, in the predominantly rural central region, eight local authorities have worked together through their cross-border partnership for over a decade to bring world-class connectivity with ultrafast broadband to the area (ICBAN, 2016). The resilience, ambition and innovation demonstrated through local and regional government across the border region in the face of both persistent and unexpected challenges are cause for optimism. Even as the practical and symbolic significance of the Irish border grows once more, nothing can alter the fact that it is a line of connection. John McGahern (2005: 270) was right: 'The pull of life [is] too great.'

Notes

1.   I cannot resist pointing out that the UK Border Strategy describes the UK border as having '270 recognised crossing points', despite the fact that the Ireland/Northern border alone has 208 roads, 2 car/passenger ferries and a

railway crossing (DTTaS & DfI, 2018; HMG, 2020b: 10). It references a report by the National Audit Office which elaborates: 'The UK border can be crossed by sea, air or rail at 113 major entry points' (NAO, 2017: 8). This is somewhat bemusing to those who drive or walk across it several times a day.

2.   This is where some proposals for an alternative to the Protocol fall down. The model of 'mutual enforcement', for example, allows for a situation of divergence between the rules UK–EU and thus that apply either side of the border (CFBP, 2021). However, it offers no assurance that there is any knowledge of precisely what crosses the border. Instead, the focus is on catching the illegal sales of products from the other side, and charging the exporter. This is, in effect, to have zero management of a hard border.

3.   One was by the legal expert, John Temple-Lang (2017), with an analysis of the impact of Brexit on the British–Irish relationship. Another was on the subject of the Good Friday Agreement, which I co-authored with my esteemed colleague David Phinnemore (2017).

4.   The quest for an alternative to the backstop centred on the fact that the backstop proposal was to avoid a hard Irish border through UK participation in the EU's customs territory and by conformity to EU single market legislation in Northern Ireland. Thus, if the backstop was fully in place, the working assumption would be that goods crossing the Irish border met the criteria for doing so. While unionists objected to the differential arrangements for Northern Ireland, the majority of Conservative politicians opposed it for putting fetters on the UK's independent trade policy.

5.   There are occasional stories about Prime Minister Boris Johnson's intention to build a bridge across, or dig a tunnel under, the Irish Sea. While expressly intended to 'delight unionists' and 'unblock Brexit tensions', this would not radically change the dynamics of the situation, given that this would create but one additional entry/exit point across the Irish Sea – still 200 fewer than across the Irish land border (Hope, 2021).

6.   Another type of technology that is of growing implementation at border entry points (though typically airports) is facial recognition. This technology is of extremely limited use when it comes to customs facilitation; it can be another means of verification, in this case verification that the driver is the one authorised to be associated with that consignment and vehicle. The use of facial recognition technology requires physical infrastructure. It also requires consent.

7.   For those who claim that the Protocol on Ireland/Northern Ireland breaches the principle of consent, the judgment of the UK Supreme Court that this principle 'neither regulated any other change in the constitutional status of Northern Ireland nor required the consent of a majority of the people of Northern Ireland

to the withdrawal of the United Kingdom from the European Union' may be enlightening (UKSC, 2017).

8. I should disclose that I am a member of this group, and I am also on the steering committee of the ARINS project.

9. At the moment, birth within the territory of Northern Ireland (or the UK) does not automatically qualify you for British (or Irish) citizenship; you also need to have at least one parent with British or Irish citizenship. If you are born outside the UK, you need a parent with British (not Irish citizenship). Although Northern Ireland would be outside the UK after Irish unification, it would still logically be necessary to allow British citizenship to those born in Northern Ireland with parents who are Irish citizens – given that the choice to be Irish or British would remain the birthright of all born in the six counties.

10. This has been the case every year since this question was first asked in the Northern Ireland Life and Times (NILT) Survey in 2007.

11. In 2002, First Minister David Trimble described the Republic of Ireland as a 'pathetic, sectarian, mono-ethnic, mono-cultural state'. Such a description of Ireland belongs firmly in the past.

12. For instance, in December 2020, the Taoiseach Micheál Martin commented in the Dáil: 'what we're witnessing in Northern Ireland could happen here if we allow things to go out of control – which we're not going to do'. And the Labour Leader, Alan Kelly, echoed his sentiments in warning that the approach taken in Northern Ireland to the crisis 'has consequences for us all in the rest of this island' (Martin, 2020).

5

conclusion

We want Northern Ireland's place in the UK internal market restored.
I think that's fairly basic and simple. I wish someone could show me any
other example in the world where you have this kind of border right
down the middle of a country, an internal border within a country that
separates one part of the country from the other. And that simply is not
acceptable. (Donaldson, 2021)

Surveys taken 20 years after the Good Friday (Belfast) Agreement indicated that a majority of people in Northern Ireland were not likely to vote for a united Ireland in any future referendum. A majority of people in Northern Ireland had voted to remain in the European Union, and a majority of people – of all backgrounds – wanted the UK to have a 'close relationship' with the EU after Brexit (Garry et al., 2018; NILT, 2019). Put together, this suggests that the majority of people in Northern Ireland were relatively comfortable with the status quo pre-Brexit. But after Brexit, and 100 years after partition, that status quo has been vigorously shaken. Historical experience from Ireland/Northern Ireland has already shown that international agreements do not bring resolution, only consequences that have to be enacted and managed. Any new border regime is but the working out of a changed legal, economic and, on occasion, political relationship between two states. This is true of the Ireland/Northern Ireland Protocol. There has been a hardening of borders all around Northern Ireland because of the changed legal conditions for movement across them. Whether it be for the movement of pets or plants or mobile phones or migrant workers, these controls make the borders around Northern Ireland seem friction-filled. And the friction is not confined to inconvenience and costs.

With complication and upheaval comes insecurity, and with this comes a retreat to the most trusted moorings. In times of flux in Northern Ireland, the two main political ideologies coalesce around opposing pillars. The perils for the 'common ground' in Northern Ireland lie in the nature of the post-Brexit environment. The whole process of Brexit is about adding friction and separation where there was none before. Northern Ireland is closely integrated with both Ireland and Great Britain, across land and sea. A process of dis-integration, no matter how limited, has inevitably disturbed the fragile political consensus. The Protocol brings friction and separation across both borders. It is a compromise in which, one might say, 'parity of esteem' was shown to both unionism and nationalism. Both are, to no small degree, affronted. Nationalists see the alternative to this flux in plain terms: 'Irish unity: the solution to Brexit'. The reaction from some unionists has been equally blunt: 'Kill the Protocol or kill the Union'. The chagrin of unionists is epitomised in the unfortunately myopic comments of DUP MP Jeffrey Donaldson (quoted above). What is particularly alarming for unionists is that the security of unionism depended on the continuation of the status quo. While nationalists want to see change to Northern Ireland's state, unionists, by definition, do not. Indeed, if there was to be a united Ireland, what would be the point of unionism as a political aspiration? There would be no prospect of another referendum on the future status of Northern Ireland, let alone any chance of winning one. And so, in these times of tumult, the temptation for unionists is to place as much weight as possible on the furthest counterbalance to nationalism. Some, such as former First Minister Peter Robinson (2021), have claimed that unionists face a choice between the Protocol or Stormont. Unionist refusal to participate in the Assembly and Executive would not, in the strictest sense, make a jot of difference to the operation of the Protocol, but it would constitute a blow to another international agreement, namely the one made in 1998. This, of course, would not come as a regret to everyone, and especially not to some loyalists. Why share power in Northern Ireland if London could provide a straightforward counterweight to Dublin? The answer, of course, is that no British government is likely to be either willing or able to play this part.

For the reasons elaborated throughout the course of this book, the constitutional status of Northern Ireland – and with it the nature of the Irish border – is no uni-dimensional or domestic matter, for either London or Dublin. Although some unionists are wary of the cross-border dimensions of the 1998 Agreement, these are the very same elements which could provide them with the means not only to imagine a post-unity future but to shape it. The Agreement embodies and protects the principle of integration between these islands. Its east/west institutions and structures offer a basis for evolution and adaptation. In this way, instead of turning back to the 1800 Act of Union or to the 1912 Ulster Covenant as a guide, unionism might be better advised to turn to the 1998 Agreement. Therein lies the means of finding 'common policies and common action' between the regions and nations of these islands, even if that includes an independent Scotland and a united Ireland. As such, the Agreement should not be considered as document for Northern Ireland alone. It is of fundamental importance to the future of Great Britain as well as Ireland. Furthermore, it recognises that borders can be hard for some things (e.g. state jurisdiction) and soft for others (e.g. water pollution, language, tourism) at the same time. This has new potential in the present day. For many people in Northern Ireland, the fact that state borders exemplify the limitations of state sovereignty is not a reason to press for an expansion of that sovereignty but rather stimulus for the transnational action needed to address the issues that matter most. The Agreement's architecture of cross-border cooperation and governance offer the means by which to identify and meet common concerns across the island of Ireland and the Irish Sea. Such means have become all the more important now. Equally imperative is faithful adherence to the values underpinning it all:

> We are committed to partnership, equality and mutual respect as the basis of relationships within Northern Ireland, between North and South, and between these islands.

After all, the 'unique circumstances on the island of Ireland' did not begin with the Irish border, and neither will they end with it.

references

@BorderIrish (2019) *I am the Irish Border, so I am*. London: HarperCollins.

Adamson, I. (1987) *The Identity of Ulster: The land, the language, and the people*. Newtownards, Co. Down: Pretani Press.

Adamson, I. (1998) *Dalaradia, Kingdom of the Cruthin*. Newtownards, Co. Down: Pretani Press.

All-Party Anti-Partition Conference (1950) *Ireland's Right to Unity*. Dublin: Browne and Nolan.

Anderson, J. and O'Dowd, L. (1999) Borders, border regions and territoriality: Contradictory meanings, changing significance. *Regional Studies*, 33(7), 593–604.

Anderson, M. and Bort, E. (1999) *The Irish Border: History, politics, culture*. Liverpool: Liverpool University Press.

Arthur, P. (2000) *Special Relationships: Britain, Ireland and the Northern Ireland problem*. Belfast: Blackstaff Press.

Bhreathnach, E. (2018) Communities and their landscapes, in Smith, B. (ed.), *The Cambridge History of Ireland*. Cambridge: Cambridge University Press, pp. 15–46.

Bradley, J. and Best, M. (2012) Bypassed places? The post-Belfast Agreement border region economy. *Journal of Cross-Border Studies*, 6, 45–58.

Bradley, J. and Birnie, E. (2001) *Can the Celtic Tiger cross the Irish Border?* Cork: Cork University Press.

Brambilla, C., Laine, J.P. and Bocchi, G. (eds) (2015) *Borderscaping: Imaginations and practices of border making*. London: Routledge.

Breen, S. (2021) Gavin Robinson right to warn of border poll: DUP MPs. *Belfast Telegraph*, 18 January 2021 (www.belfasttelegraph.co.uk/news/politics/gavin-robinson-right-to-warn-of-border-poll-dup-mps-39983640.html).

Brokenshire, J. (2016) Difficult to see how NI can stay in the EU. *BBC News*, 18 July 2016 (www.bbc.co.uk/news/uk-northern-ireland-36824749).

Buchanan, S. (2014) *Transforming Conflict through Social and Economic Development: Practice and policy lessons from Northern Ireland and the border counties*. Manchester: Manchester University Press.

Butler, G. and Barrett, G. (2018) Europe's 'other' open-border zone: The Common Travel Area under the shadow of Brexit. *Cambridge Yearbook of European Legal Studies*, 20, 252–286.

Byrne, S., Skarlato, O., Fissuh, E. and Irvin, C. (2009) Building trust and goodwill in Northern Ireland and the border counties: The impact of economic aid on the peace process. *Irish Political Studies*, 24(3), 337–363.

Carr, G. (2017) *The Rule of the Land: Walking Ireland's border*. London: Faber & Faber.

CBI NI (2018) *All Together Better: Accessible labour – a necessity for regional economic prosperity*. Confederation of British Industry, Northern Ireland, September 2018 (www.cbi.org.uk/articles/all-together-better/).

CEC (2018) *European Commission draft Withdrawal Agreement on the withdrawal of the United Kingdom of Great Britain and Northern Ireland from the European Union and the European Atomic Energy Community*. European Commission, 28 February 2018 (https://ec.europa.eu/info/sites/info/files/draft_withdrawal_agreement.pdf).

CFBP (2021) *Correcting the Damage caused by the Northern Ireland Protocol: How mutual enforcement can solve the Northern Ireland border problem*. Centre for Brexit Policy, February 2021 (https://centreforbrexitpolicy.org.uk/wp-content/uploads/2021/02/Correcting-the-Damage-Caused-by-the-Northern-Ireland-Protocol-5-Feb-21.pdf).

Coakley, J. (2017) Adjusting to partition: From irredentism to 'consent' in twentieth-century Ireland. *Irish Studies Review*, 25(2), 193–214.

Coakley, J. and Laffan, B. (2005) Institutions and modes of territorial management: The challenge of British-Irish studies, in Coakley, J. et al. (eds), *Renovation or Revolution? New territorial politics in Ireland and the United Kingdom*. Dublin: University College Dublin Press, pp. 200–221.

Coakley, J. and O'Dowd, L. (2007) The 'new' Irish border: Changing political, economic and social dimensions, in Coakley, J. and O'Dowd, L. (eds), *Crossing the Border: New relationships between Northern Ireland and the Republic of Ireland*. Dublin: Irish Academic Press, pp. 3–28.

Coakley, J, Laffan, B. and Todd, J. (eds) (2005) *Renovation or Revolution? New territorial politics in Ireland and the United Kingdom*. Dublin: University College Dublin Press.

Cochrane, F. (2020) *Breaking Peace: Brexit and Northern Ireland*. Manchester: Manchester University Press.

Coleman, M. (2014) *The Irish Revolution, 1916–1923*. London: Routledge.

Costello, F. (1988) Lloyd George and Ireland, 1919–1921: An uncertain policy. *Canadian Journal of Irish Studies*, 14(1), 5–16.

CSO (2017) *Census 2016 Summary Results*. Dublin: Central Statistics Office (www.cso.ie/en/media/csoie/releasespublications/documents/population/2017/Chapter_5_Diversity.pdf).

Daly, M.E. (1992) *Industrial Development and Irish National Identity, 1922–1939*. New York: Syracuse University Press.

D'Arcy, M. and Dickson, T. (1995) *Border Crossings: Developing Ireland's island economy*. Dublin: Gill & Macmillan.

Davies, G. (2020) Facilitating cross-border criminal justice cooperation between the UK and Ireland after Brexit: 'Keeping the lights on' to ensure the safety of the Common Travel Area. *Journal of Criminal Law*. doi:10.1177/0022018320977528

Delaney, E. (2001) Irish migration to Britain, 1939–1945. *Irish Economic and Social History*, 28, 47–71.

de Mars, S., Murray, C., Donoghue, A. and Warwick, B. (2018) *Bordering Two Unions: Northern Ireland and Brexit*. Bristol: Policy Press.

Department of the Taoiseach (2020) *Shared Island* (www.gov.ie/en/publication/de9fc-shared-island/).

DFA (1972) *Ireland North and South in the EEC*. Department of Foreign Affairs, Ireland.

Donaldson, J. (2021) Jeffrey Donaldson, DUP MP interview on Evening Extra. *BBC Radio Ulster,* 2 February 2021 (www.bbc.co.uk/sounds/play/m000rv4y).

Dooley, T.A.M. (1994) From the Belfast Boycott to the Boundary Commission: Fears and hopes in County Monaghan, 1920–26. *Clogher Record*, 15(1), 90–106.

Dorney, J. (2019) The making of the Irish border, 1912–1925: A short history. *The Irish Story* (www.theirishstory.com/2019/09/12/the-making-of-the-irish-border-1912-1925-a-short-history/#_edn9).

DTTaS & DfI (2018) *Public road border crossings between the Republic of Ireland and Northern Ireland*. Department of Transport, Tourism and Sport (Republic of Ireland) and Department for Infrastructure (Northern Ireland) (www.infrastructure-ni.gov.uk/sites/default/files/publications/infrastructure/border-crossing-joint-report-final_0.pdf).

Duffy, S. (1995) The first Ulster Plantation: John de Courcy and the men of Cumbria, in Barry, T. et al. (eds), *Colony and Frontier in Medieval Ireland: Essays presented to J. F. Lydon*. London: Hambledon Press, pp. 1–27.

DUP (2021) *Free us from the Protocol: A five point plan*. Democratic Unionist
Party, 2 February 2021 (https://mydup.com/news/dup-free-us-from-protocol).

EC & HMG (2017) *Joint report from the negotiators of the European Union and
the United Kingdom Government on progress during phase 1 of negotiations
under Article 50 TEU on the United Kingdom's orderly withdrawal from the
European Union*. European Council and Her Majesty's Government (https://
ec.europa.eu/commission/sites/beta-political/files/joint_report.pdf).

EC & HMG (2018) *Withdrawal Agreement and Political Declaration on the future
relationship between the UK and the EU as endorsed by leaders at a special
meeting of the European Council*. European Council and Her Majesty's
Government, 25 November 2018 (www.gov.uk/government/publications/
withdrawal-agreement-and-political-declaration).

EC & HMG (2019a) *Mapping exercise of North-South cooperation*. European Council
and Her Majesty's Government, June 2019 (https://ec.europa.eu/commission/
sites/beta-political/files/mapping_of_north-south_cooperation_0.pdf).

EC & HMG (2019b) *The revised Withdrawal Agreement and Political Declaration
considered and agreed at European Council*. European Council and Her
Majesty's Government, 17 October 2019 (www.gov.uk/government/
publications/new-withdrawal-agreement-and-political-declaration).

EC & HMG (2020) *Trade and Cooperation Agreement between the European
Union and European Atomic Energy Community, of the one part, and the
United Kingdom of Great Britain and Northern Ireland, of the other part*.
European Council and Her Majesty's Government, 24 December 2020
(https://ec.europa.eu/info/sites/info/files/draft_eu-uk_trade_and_cooperation_
agreement.pdf).

ECOSOC (1983) *Irish Border Areas: Information report*. Economic and Social
Committee of the European Community (http://aei.pitt.edu/41825/1/A5968.
pdf).

Electoral Commission (2018) *Digital Campaigning: Increasing transparency for
voters*. Electoral Commission (www.electoralcommission.org.uk/media/1831).

Ellis, S.G. (1985) *Tudor Ireland. Crown, community and the conflict of cultures
1470–1603*. London: Longman.

European Council (2017) *European Council (Art. 50) guidelines for Brexit
negotiations*. European Council, 29 April 2017 (www.consilium.europa.eu/en/
meetings/european-council/2017/04/29/).

Fanning, R. (2001) Playing it cool: The response of the British and Irish
governments to the outbreak of the Troubles in Northern Ireland, 1968–9. *Irish
Studies in International Affairs*, 12, 57–85.

Ferriter, D. (2019). *The Border: The legacy of a century of Anglo-Irish politics*. London: Profile Books.

FitzGerald, G. (1982) Reconciliation in a divided community. Heinz Fellowship Lecture delivered by the leader of Fine Gael, University of Pittsburgh, 30 September 1982, cited in Hayward, K. (2009) *Irish Nationalism and European Integration*. Manchester: Manchester University Press, p. 157.

FitzGerald, J. and Kenny, S. (2020) "Till debt do us part": Financial implications of the divorce of the Irish Free State from the United Kingdom, 1922–1926. *European Review of Economic History,* 24(4), 818–842.

Fitzpatrick, D. (1996) Militarism in Ireland, 1900–1922, in Bartlett, T. and Jeffery, K.A. (eds), *Military History of Ireland*. Cambridge: Cambridge University Press, pp. 383–386.

Foster, A. (2013) Border poll considered by DUP, says Foster. *BBC News*, 22 January 2013 (www.bbc.co.uk/news/uk-northern-ireland-21140469).

Foster, A. (2017) Put border poll off 'for generations', says DUP's Foster. *BBC News*, 31 May 2017 (www.bbc.co.uk/news/uk-northern-ireland-40104316).

Frame, R. (2018) Contexts, divisions and unities: Perspectives from the later middle ages, in Smith, B. (ed.), *The Cambridge History of Ireland*. Cambridge: Cambridge University Press, pp. 523–550.

Fraser, T.G. (1984) *Partition in Ireland, India and Palestine: Theory and practice*. London: Macmillan.

Garry, J., McNicholl, K., O'Leary, B. and Pow, J. (2018) *Northern Ireland and the UK's exit from the EU: What do people think?* UK in a Changing Europe, May 2018 (www.qub.ac.uk/sites/brexitni/BrexitandtheBorder/Report/).

Garvin, T. (1981) *The Evolution of Irish Nationalist Politics*. Dublin: Gill & Macmillan.

Geoghegan, P. (2020) *Democracy for Sale: Dark money and dirty politics*. London: Head of Zeus.

Government of Ireland & HMG (2019) *Memorandum of understanding concerning the Common Travel Area and associated reciprocal rights and privileges*. Government of Ireland and Her Majesty's Government, 8 May 2019 (https://assets.publishing.service.gov.uk/government/uploads/system/uploads/attachment_data/file/800280/CTA-MoU-UK.pdf).

Gwynn, D. (1932) *The Life of John Redmond*. London: Harper.

Hansard (1914) *Government of Ireland (Amendment) Bill, HC Bill 326*, 15 July 1914 (https://archive.org/stream/op1256356-1001#page/n1/mode/2up).

Hansard (1972) Debate on Northern Ireland, *HC Deb*, 24 March 1972, Vol. 833 col. 1859 (https://api.parliament.uk/historic-hansard/commons/1972/mar/24/northern-ireland).

Harguindéguy, J.-B. and Hayward, K. (2014) The institutionalization of the European internal cross-border co-operation policy: A first appraisal. *European Planning Studies*, 22(1), 184–203.

Harris, R. (1972) *Prejudice and Tolerance in Ulster: A study of neighbours and 'strangers' in a border community*. Manchester: Manchester University Press.

Hayward, K. (2007) Mediating the European ideal: Cross-border programmes and conflict resolution on the island of Ireland. *JCMS: Journal of Common Market Studies*, 45(3), 675–693.

Hayward, K. (2017) *Bordering on Brexit: Views from local communities in the central border region of Ireland/Northern Ireland*. Irish Central Border Area Network and Queen's University Belfast, November 2017 (www.qub.ac.uk/brexit/Brexitfilestore/Filetoupload,781170,en.pdf).

Hayward, K. (2018) *Brexit at the Border: Voices of local communities in the central border region of Ireland/Northern Ireland*. Irish Central Border Area Network and Queen's University Belfast, June 2018 (www.qub.ac.uk/brexit/Brexitfilestore/Filetoupload,824444,en.pdf).

Hayward, K. and Komarova, M. (2019) *The Border into Brexit: Perspectives from local communities in the central border region of Ireland/Northern Ireland*. Irish Central Border Area Network and Queen's University Belfast, September 2019 (https://ukandeu.ac.uk/wp-content/uploads/2019/12/The-Border-into-Brexit-perspectives-from-local-communities-in-the-central-border-region-of-Ireland-and-Northern-Ireland.pdf).

Hayward, K. and Magennis, E. (2014) The business of building peace: Private sector cooperation across the Irish border. *Irish Political Studies*, 29(1), 154–175.

Hayward, K, Phinnemore, D. and Komarova, M. (2020) *Anticipating and meeting new multilevel governance challenges in Northern Ireland after Brexit*. UK in a Changing Europe, May 2020 (https://ukandeu.ac.uk/research-papers/anticipating-and-meeting-new-multilevel-governance-challenges-in-northern-ireland-after-brexit/).

Healy, C. (1945) *The Mutilation of a Nation: The story of the partition of Ireland*. Derry: Derry Journal Ltd.

Hegel, G.W.F. (2005) *Philosophy of Right* (trans. S.W. Dyde). New York: Dover Publications (1st edn, 1821).

Hennessey, T. (1998) *Dividing Ireland: World War One and partition*. London: Routledge.

Heslinga, M.W. (1971) *The Irish Border as a Cultural Divide: A contribution to the study of regionalism in the British Isles*. Assen, the Netherlands: Van Gorcum.

HMG (2017a) *Prime Minister's speech on the Government's negotiating objectives,* Lancaster House. Her Majesty's Government, 17 January 2017 (www.gov.uk/government/speeches/the-governments-negotiating-objectives-for-exiting-the-eu-pm-speech).

HMG (2017b) *The Prime Minister's letter to Donald Tusk triggering Article 50.* Her Majesty's Government, 29 March 2017 (www.gov.uk/government/publications/prime-ministers-letter-to-donald-tusk-triggering-article-50/prime-ministers-letter-to-donald-tusk-triggering-article-50).

HMG (2017c) *Confidence and supply agreement between the Conservative and Unionist Party and the Democratic Unionist Party.* Her Majesty's Government, 26 June 2017 (www.gov.uk/government/publications/conservative-and-dup-agreement-and-uk-government-financial-support-for-northern-ireland/agreement-between-the-conservative-and-unionist-party-and-the-democratic-unionist-party-on-support-for-the-government-in-parliament).

HMG (2020a) *The UK's approach to the Northern Ireland Protocol*. Command Paper 226. Her Majesty's Government, 20 May 2020 (www.gov.uk/government/publications/the-uks-approach-to-the-northern-ireland-protocol).

HMG (2020b) *2025 UK Border Strategy*. Command Paper 352. Cabinet Office, Her Majesty's Government, December 2020 (https://assets.publishing.service.gov.uk/government/uploads/system/uploads/attachment_data/file/945380/2025_UK_Border_Strategy.pdf).

HMSO (1920) *Government of Ireland Act.* His Majesty's Stationery Office, 23 December 1920 (www.legislation.gov.uk/ukpga/1920/67/pdfs/ukpga_19200067_en.pdf).

Hope, C. (2021) 'Boris' Burrow tunnel' to Northern Ireland set to get green light. *Sunday Telegraph*, 14 February 2021 (www.telegraph.co.uk/politics/2021/02/13/boris-burrow-tunnel-northern-ireland-set-get-green-light/).

Hopkinson, M. (1988) *Green against Green: The Irish Civil War*. Dublin: Gill & Macmillan.

Humphreys, R. (2018) *Beyond the Border: The Good Friday Agreement and Irish unity after Brexit*. Newbridge, Co. Kildare: Merrion Press.

ICBAN (2016) *Fibre at a Crossroads: Infrastructure solutions for high speed internet in the central border region of Northern Ireland/Ireland*. Irish Central Border Area Network, June 2016 (https://icban.com/site/wp-content/uploads/2018/03/Fibre-at-a-Crossroads-Part-I-Exec-Summary-Jun-16.pdf).

ICR (2018) *Report of the Independent Commission on Referendums*. Independent Commission on Referendums, The Constitution Unit, University College London, July 2018 (www.ucl.ac.uk/constitution-unit/sites/constitution-unit/files/ICR_Final_Report.pdf).

Jackson, A. (1989) *The Ulster Party. Irish unionists in the House of Commons, 1884–1911*. Oxford: Clarendon Press.

Jackson, A. (2003) *Home Rule: An Irish History 1800–2000*. London: Weidenfeld & Nicolson.

Karlsson, L. (2017) *Smart Border 2.0: Avoiding a hard border on the island of Ireland for customs control and the free movement of persons*. Policy Department for Citizens' Rights and Constitutional Affairs, European Parliament, November 2017 (www.europarl.europa.eu/RegData/etudes/STUD/2017/596828/IPOL_STU%282017%29596828_EN.pdf).

Kennedy, M. (2000) *Division and Consensus: The politics of cross-border relations in Ireland, 1925–1969*. Dublin: Institute of Public Administration.

Kenny, E. (2016) Border poll: Enda Kenny 'Brexit talks must consider possibility'. *BBC News*, 18 July 2016 (www.bbc.co.uk/news/uk-northern-ireland-36830452).

Laffan, M. (1983) *The Partition of Ireland, 1911–1925*. Dublin: Dublin Historical Association.

League of Nations (1924) *Treaty between Great Britain and Ireland*, 6 December 1921. League of Nations treaty series No. 636, 1924 (https://treaties.un.org/doc/Publication/UNTS/LON/Volume%2026/v26.pdf#page=9).

Leary, P. (2016) *Unapproved Routes: Histories of the Irish border, 1922–72*. Oxford: Oxford University Press.

Leary, P. (2018) A house divided: The Murrays of the border and the rise and decline of a small Irish house. *History Workshop Journal*, 86, 269–290.

Lewis, G. (2005) *Carson: The man who divided Ireland*. London: Hambledon Continuum.

Longford, F.P. and O'Neill, T.P. (1970) *Eamonn De Valera*. Dublin: Gill & Macmillan, in association with Hutchinson.

Lynch, J. (1971) Speech by the Taoiseach, Dundalk, 28 May 1971, in *Irish Unity: Northern Ireland and Anglo-Irish relations, speeches August 1969–October 1971*. Dublin: Government of Ireland Information Bureau, pp. 55–59.

Lynch, R. (2019) *The Partition of Ireland, 1918–1925*. Cambridge: Cambridge University Press.

MacNeill, E. (1920) *Phases of Irish History*. Dublin: M.H. Gill & Son.

Mallory, J.P. (2013) *The Origins of the Irish*. London: Thames and Hudson.

Mansergh, N. (1978) *The Prelude to Partition: Concepts and aims in Ireland and India*. Cambridge: Cambridge University Press.

Martin, M. (2020) Covid situation in Northern Ireland 'very worrying' – Martin. *Irish Times,* 16 December 2020 (www.irishtimes.com/news/politics/oireachtas/covid-situation-in-northern-ireland-very-worrying-martin-1.4438589).

May, T. (2018) Oral Answers to Questions – Prime Minister – in the House of Commons, 28 February 2018. *Hansard*, Vol. 636, col. 825 (https://hansard.parliament.uk/Commons/2018-02-28/debates/E91093BE-192E-4E01-ABCE-3CEB6973074B/PrimeMinister).

McClelland, A. and Duffy, M. (2019) *Northern Ireland businesses: Trade flows, surplus and deficit*. Department for the Economy, Northern Ireland, 26 September 2019 (www.economy-ni.gov.uk/publications/northern-ireland-businesses-trade-flows-surplus-and-deficit).

McClements, F. and Bray, J. (2021) Coronavirus: 11 further deaths and 504 new cases recorded in North. *Irish Times*, 3 February 2021 (www.irishtimes.com/news/health/coronavirus-11-further-deaths-and-504-new-cases-recorded-in-north-1.4475024).

McGahern, J. (2005) *Memoir.* London: Faber & Faber.

McNicholl, K., Stevenson, C. and Garry, J. (2019) How the 'Northern Irish' national identity is understood and used by young people and politicians. *Political Psychology*, 40(3), 487–505.

Moloney, E. (2007) *A Secret History of the IRA*. London: Penguin.

Moore, C. (2019) *Birth of the Border: The impact of partition in Ireland*. Newbridge, Co. Kildare: Merrion Press.

Morgan, H. (1993) *Tyrone's Rebellion: The outbreak of the Nine Years War in Tudor Ireland.* Woodbridge: Boydell and Brewer.

Moxon-Browne, E. (1991) National identity in Northern Ireland, in Stringer, P. and Robinson, G. (eds), *Social Attitudes in Northern Ireland*. Belfast: Blackstaff Press, pp. 23–30.

Mulroe, P. (2017) *Bombs, Bullets and the Border. Policing Ireland's frontier: Irish security policy, 1969–1978*. Newbridge, Co. Kildare: Irish Academic Press.

Murphy, M.C. (2018) *Europe and Northern Ireland's Future: Negotiating Brexit's unique case*. Newcastle upon Tyne: Agenda Publishing.

Murray, D. (1999) *A Register of Cross-Border Links in Ireland*. Limerick: Centre for Peace and Development Studies, University of Limerick.

Murray, P. (2011) *The Irish Boundary Commission and its Origins, 1886–1925*. Dublin: University College Dublin Press.

NAO (2017) *The UK Border: Issues and challenges for government's management of the border in light of the UK's planned departure from the European Union.* HC513, National Audit Office (www.nao.org.uk/wp-content/uploads/2017/10/The-UK-border.pdf).

Nash, C., Graham, B. and Reid, B. (2013) *Partitioned Lives: The Irish borderland.* London: Routledge.

NILT (2019) *Northern Ireland Life and Times Survey* (www.ark.ac.uk/nilt/results/).

NISRA (2019) *Long-term international migration statistics for Northern Ireland (2018).* Northern Ireland Statistics and Research Agency (www.nisra.gov.uk/publications/long-term-international-migration-statistics-northern-ireland-2018).

NWCBRG (1994) *Shaping the Future Together: A development programme for the north west Euro-region.* Derry: North West Region Cross Border Group.

NWRDG (2017) *Ireland 2040: Our plan.* Submission from the North West Regional Development Group as a joint committee of Donegal County Council and Derry City & Strabane District Council (https://npf.ie/wp-content/uploads/0664-North-West-Regional-Development-Group.compressed.pdf).

Ó Beacháin, D. (2019) *From Partition to Brexit: The Irish government and Northern Ireland.* Manchester: Manchester University Press.

O'Callaghan, M. (2000) Old parchment and water: The Boundary Commission of 1925 and the copperfastening of the Irish border. *Bulla'n*, 4(2), 2–55.

O'Callaghan, M. (2006) Genealogies of partition: History, history-writing and 'the Troubles' in Ireland. *Critical Review of International Social and Political Philosophy*, 9(4), 619–634.

O'Ceallaigh, D. (2019) Some thoughts on the 'Travellers' and on Maryfield, in Daly, M.E. (ed.), *Brokering the Good Friday Agreement: The untold story.* Dublin: Royal Irish Academy, pp. 83–93.

O'Dowd, L., McCall, C. and Damkat, I. (2006) Sustaining cross-border cooperation: A cross-sectoral case study approach. *Mapping Frontiers, Plotting Pathways* working paper 11. University College Dublin and Queen's University Belfast (www.cdt-piads.ac.uk/research-centres/Centrefor InternationalBordersResearch/Publications/WorkingPapers/Mapping Frontiersworkingpapers/Filetoupload,175407,en.pdf).

Ó Drisceoil, D. (2011) When Dev defaulted: The land annuities dispute, 1926–38. *History Ireland*, 19(3) (www.historyireland.com/20th-century-contemporary-history/when-dev-defaulted-the-land-annuities-dispute-1926-38/).

O'Halloran, C. (1987) *Partition and the Limits of Irish Nationalism: An ideology under stress.* Dublin: Gill & Macmillan.

O'Neill, D. (1946) *The Partition of Ireland: How and why it was accomplished*. Dublin: Gill & Sons.

Oxford Economics (2020) *The impact of changes to migration policy on the Northern Ireland economy*. Department for the Economy, Northern Ireland (www.economy-ni.gov.uk/sites/default/files/publications/economy/Impact-changes-migration-policy-ni-economy.pdf).

Paisley, I. (1985) Speech at mass rally, Belfast City Hall, 24 November 1985. Quoted in *The New York Times*, 24 November 1985 (www.nytimes.com/1985/11/24/world/huge-rally-in-belfast-protests-british-irish-accord.html).

Parker, N. and Vaughan-Williams, N. (eds) (2014) *Critical Border Studies: Broadening and deepening the 'lines in the sand' agenda*. London: Routledge.

Parkinson, A. (2012) *Friends in High Places: Ulster's resistance to Irish home rule, 1912–14*. Newtownards, Co. Down: Ulster Historical Foundation.

Patterson, G. (2019) *Backstop Land*. London: Apollo Press.

Patterson, H. (2013) *Ireland's Violent Frontier: The border and Anglo-Irish relations during the Troubles*. Basingstoke: Palgrave Macmillan.

Phinnemore, D. (2020) Democratic Consent and the Protocol on Ireland/Northern Ireland. *Queen's Policy Engagement blog*, 6 January 2020 (http://qpol.qub.ac.uk/democratic-consent-and-the-protocol-on-ireland-northern-ireland/).

Phinnemore, D. and Hayward, K. (2017) *UK Withdrawal ('Brexit') and the Good Friday Agreement*. Policy Department for Citizens' Rights and Constitutional Affairs, European Parliament, November 2017 (www.europarl.europa.eu/RegData/etudes/STUD/2017/596826/IPOL_STU(2017)596826_EN.pdf).

Phoenix, E. (2018) Idea of Dublin-Belfast economic 'corridor' floated in 1992. *Irish Times*, 2 January 2018 (www.irishtimes.com/news/ireland/irish-news/idea-of-dublin-belfast-economic-corridor-floated-in-1992-1.3340632).

Pickering, S. and Weber, L. (eds) (2006) *Borders, Mobility and Technologies of Control*. Dordrecht: Springer.

Power, P. (1997) *The Courts Martial of 1798–99*. Dublin: The Irish Historical Press.

Prosperity UK (2019) *Alternative arrangements for the Irish border: Report and protocols*. Prosperity UK, July 2019 (www.prosperity-uk.com/wp-content/uploads/sites/43/2019/07/AAC-Final-Report-and-Protocols-18-07-2019.pdf).

Rafferty, O. (1994) *Catholicism in Ulster, 1603–1983: An interpretative history*. Columbia, SC: University of South Carolina Press.

Rankin, K.J. (2005) The creation and consolidation of the Irish border. *Mapping Frontiers, Plotting Pathways* working paper 2. University College Dublin and Queen's University Belfast (www.qub.ac.uk/research-centres/

CentreforInternationalBordersResearch/Publications/WorkingPapers/
MappingFrontiersworkingpapers/Filetoupload,175395,en.pdf).

Rankin, K.J. (2006) The provenance and dissolution of the Irish Boundary
Commission. *Mapping Frontiers, Plotting Pathways* working paper 2.
University College Dublin and Queen's University Belfast (www.ucd.ie/ibis/
filestore/wp2006/79/79_kr.pdf).

Rast, M. (2019) *Shaping Ireland's Independence: Nationalist, unionist and British
solutions to the Irish Question, 1909–1925*. London: Palgrave Macmillan.

REACH (2021) *Dalaradia: Respect, Heritage, Culture*. Renewing – Engaging –
Advancing – Community – Hopes project (www.dalaradia.co.uk/?
page_id=127).

Reuters (2007) *Last of Northern Ireland's watch towers removed*, 13 February
2007 (www.reuters.com/article/uk-irish-tower/last-of-northern-irelands-
watch-towers-removed-idUKL1325533820070213).

Robinson, G. (2021a) Senior DUP MP Gavin Robinson warns unionism to
prepare for border poll. *Irish News*, 18 January 2021 (www.irishnews.com/
news/northernirelandnews/2021/01/18/news/gavin-robinson-echoes-
dup-namesake-s-call-for-unionism-to-get-ready-for-a-border-poll-2189559/).

Robinson, G. (2021b) DUP MP: Garda's new fines for crossing into the Republic
are 'awkward for no hard border brigade'. *News Letter*, 5 February 2020
(www.newsletter.co.uk/news/politics/dup-mp-gardas-new-fines-crossing-
republic-are-awkward-no-hard-border-brigade-3126375).

Robinson, P. (2021) Unionists might face a choice between keeping Stormont or
scrapping the Irish Sea border. *News Letter*, 12 February 2021 (www.
newsletter.co.uk/news/opinion/peter-robinson-unionists-might-face-choice-
between-keeping-stormont-or-scrapping-irish-sea-border-3132423).

Rose, R. (1971) *Governing without Consensus: An Irish perspective*. London:
Faber & Faber.

Ryan, B. (2001) The Common Travel Area between Britain and Ireland. *Modern
Law Review*, 64(6), 855–874.

Sassen, S. (2006) *Territory, Authority, Rights: From medieval to global
assemblages*. Princeton, NJ: Princeton University Press.

Scott, J.W. (ed.) (2020) *A Research Agenda for Border Studies*. Northampton,
MA: Edward Elgar.

Smyth, J. (2000) The Act of Union and public opinion, in Smyth, J. (ed.),
Revolution, Counter-Revolution and Union: Ireland in the 1790s. Cambridge:
Cambridge University Press, pp. 146–160.

Staunton, D. and Leahy, P. (2017) Brexit summit: EU accepts united Ireland declaration. *Irish Times*, 29 April 2017 (www.irishtimes.com/news/world/europe/brexit-summit-eu-accepts-united-ireland-declaration-1.3066569).

Stewart, A.T.Q. (1967) *The Ulster Crisis: Resistance to Home Rule, 1912–14.* London: Faber & Faber.

Tannam, E. (1999) *Cross-Border Cooperation in the Republic of Ireland and Northern Ireland*. Basingstoke: Palgrave Macmillan.

Tannam, E. (2006) Cross-border co-operation between Northern Ireland and the Republic of Ireland: Neo-functionalism revisited. *British Journal of Politics & International Relations,* 8(2), 256–276.

Temple-Lang, J. (2017) *Brexit and Ireland: Legal, political and economic considerations*. Policy Department for Citizens' Rights and Constitutional Affairs, European Parliament, November 2017 (www.europarl.europa.eu/RegData/etudes/STUD/2017/596825/IPOL_STU%282017%29596825_EN.pdf).

TEO (2016) *Letter to the Prime Minister, The Rt Hon Theresa May MP*. The Executive Office, Northern Ireland, 10 August 2016 (www.executiveoffice-ni.gov.uk/sites/default/files/publications/execoffice/Letter%20to%20PM%20from%20FM%20%26%20dFM.pdf).

Tóibín, C. (1987) *Walking along the Border*. London: Macdonald.

Tonge, J. and Gomez, R. (2015) Shared identity and the end of conflict? How far has a common sense of 'Northern Irishness' replaced British or Irish allegiances since the 1998 Good Friday Agreement? *Irish Political Studies*, 30(2), 276–298.

Trimble, D. (2002) Trimble calls for a poll on union with republic. *Observer*, 10 March 2002 (www.theguardian.com/uk/2002/mar/10/northernireland).

TUV (2021) Traditional Unionist Voice spokesperson, cited in DUP vows to send 'strong message' to Irish government over NI Protocol. *BBC News*, 2 February 2021 (www.bbc.co.uk/news/uk-northern-ireland-55910506).

UKSC (2017) *R (on the application of Miller and another) (Respondents) v Secretary of State for Exiting the European Union (Appellant)*, Supreme Court Judgment, UKSC 2016/0196, 24 January 2017 (www.supremecourt.uk/cases/docs/uksc-2016-0196-judgment.pdf).

UUEPC (2017) *Brexit and the Border Corridor on the island of Ireland: Risks, opportunities and issues to consider*. Ulster University Economic Policy Centre (www.ulster.ac.uk/__data/assets/pdf_file/0008/477854/Border_Corridor_Brexit-report-120914-web.pdf).

Villiers, T. (2016) Villiers says Brexit would not undermine peace process. *Irish Times*, 9 June 2016 (www.irishtimes.com/news/politics/villiers-says-brexit-would-not-undermine-peace-process-1.2678138).

Walker, B. (2005) The 1885 and 1886 general elections in Ireland. *History Ireland*, 13(6) (www.historyireland.com/18th-19th-century-history/the-1885-and-1886-general-elections-in-ireland/).

WGURII (2020) *Interim Report of the Working Group on Unification Referendums on the island of Ireland.* The Constitution Unit, University College London, November 2020 (www.ucl.ac.uk/constitution-unit/sites/constitution-unit/files/wgurii_interim_report_nov_2020.pdf).

Wilson, T. and Donnan, H. (2012) *A Companion to Border Studies*. Oxford: Blackwell.

index